AN EVALUATION
OF LEVEL OF ASPIRATION
AS A TRAINING PROCEDURE

1963 Award Winner

THE FORD FOUNDATION DOCTORAL
DISSERTATION SERIES

AN EVALUATION
OF LEVEL OF ASPIRATION
AS A TRAINING PROCEDURE

FORREST W. FRYER

Manpower Planning Administrator
Xerox Corporation

P R E N T I C E - H A L L ,   I N C .
Englewood Cliffs, N. J.

1960 Award Winners

Bernard H. Baum *Decentralization of Authority in a Bureaucracy*
Dissertation submitted to Department of Sociology, University of Chicago

Leon V. Hirsch *Marketing in an Underdeveloped Economy: The North Indian Sugar Industry*
Dissertation submitted to Graduate School of Business Administration, Harvard University

Bedros Peter Pashigian *The Distribution of Automobiles, an Economic Analysis of the Franchise System*
Dissertation submitted to Department of Economics, Massachusetts Institute of Technology

Martin Patchen *The Choice of Wage Comparison*
Dissertation submitted to Department of Social Psychology, University of Michigan

Fred M. Tonge *A Heuristic Program for Assembly Line Balancing*
Dissertation submitted to Graduate School of Industrial Administration, Carnegie Institute of Technology

1959 Award Winners

Kalman J. Cohen *Computer Models of the Shoe, Leather, Hide Sequence*
Dissertation submitted to Graduate School of Industrial Administration, Carnegie Institute of Technology

Bob R. Holdren *The Structure of a Retail Market and the Market Behavior of Retail Units*
Dissertation submitted to Department of Economics, Yale University

Frank Proschan *Polya Type Distributions in Renewal Theory, with an Application to an Inventory Problem*
Dissertation submitted to Department of Statistics, Stanford University

Andrew C. Stedry *Budget Control and Cost Behavior*
Dissertation submitted to Graduate School of Industrial Administration, Carnegie Institute of Technology

Victor H. Vroom *Some Personality Determinants of the Effects of Participation*
Dissertation submitted to Department of Psychology, University of Michigan

1962 Award Winners

Alexander Barges *The Effect of Capital Structure on the Cost of Capital*
  Dissertation submitted to Graduate School of Business Administration, Northwestern University

Charles P. Bonini *Simulation of Information and Decision Systems in the Firm*
  Dissertation submitted to Graduate School of Business, Carnegie Institute of Technology

James M. Ferguson *The Advertising Rate Structure in the Daily Newspaper Industry*
  Dissertation submitted to Department of Economics, University of Chicago

Gordon M. Kaufman *Statistical Decision and Related Techniques in Oil and Gas Exploration*
  Dissertation submitted to Graduate School of Business, Harvard University

H. Martin Weingartner *Mathematical Programming and the Analysis of Capital Budgeting Problems*
  Dissertation submitted to Graduate School of Industrial Administration, Carnegie Institute of Technology

1961 Award Winners

Geoffrey P. E. Clarkson *Portfolio Selection: A Simulation of Trust Investment*
  Dissertation submitted to Graduate School of Industrial Administration, Carnegie Institute of Technology

Donald E. Farrar *The Investment Decision Under Uncertainty: Portfolio Selection*
  Dissertation submitted to Faculty of Arts and Sciences, Harvard University

Richard S. Hatch *An Evaluation of a Forced-Choice Differential Accuracy Approach to the Measurement of Supervisory Empathy*
  Dissertation submitted to Department of Psychology, University of Minnesota

David Meiselman *The Term Structure of Interest Rates*
  Dissertation submitted to Department of Economics, University of Chicago

George William Summers *Financing and Initial Operations of New Firms*
  Dissertation submitted to Department of Management, Case Institute of Technology

Foreword

Dr. Fryer's dissertation, completed during the academic year 1962–1963, is one of six selected for publication in the fifth annual Doctoral Dissertation Competition sponsored by the Program in Economic Development and Administration of the Ford Foundation.

The intent of the doctoral dissertation competition has been to recognize and encourage excellence in research on business by graduate students. Publication awards, now totaling twenty-six, have been made over the five years of the competition to persons granted doctorates in business and related fields whose thesis research on problems of business was especially distinguished by its analytical content and strong roots in the underlying disciplines common to business.

In addition to Dr. Fryer's, the dissertations published this year are:

The Demand for Liquid Assets: A Temporal Cross-Section Analysis
Edgar Louis Feige
Department of Economics
University of Chicago

The Demand for Physical Capital: Application of a Wealth Model
Frederick S. Hammer
Graduate School of Industrial Administration
Carnegie Institute of Technology

The Measurement of Cumulative Advertising Effects
Kristian S. Palda
Graduate School of Business
University of Chicago

Some Large-Scale Production Scheduling Problems in the Paper Industry
John F. Pierce, Jr.
School of Industrial Management
Massachusetts Institute of Technology

The Economics of Discretionary Behavior: Managerial Objectives in a Theory of the Firm
>   Oliver E. Williamson
>   Graduate School of Industrial Administration
>   Carnegie Institute of Technology

On behalf of the Ford Foundation, I wish to express my gratitude to the members of the Editorial Committee for the care and thought they devoted to the selection process. The members of this Committee, who made the final selection of winning dissertations, were: Professor Robert Ferber of the University of Illinois, Professor Mason Haire of the University of California at Berkeley, and Professor Thomas L. Whisler of the University of Chicago.

The Editorial Committee's task was considerably lightened by the assistance of twelve readers, experts in the wide range of disciplines covered in the competition, who carefully screened the theses submitted. The Foundation joins the Committee in acknowledging their debt to Professors Paul E. Breer of Cornell University, Earl F. Cheit and Lyman W. Porter of the University of California at Berkeley, James R. Jackson of the University of California at Los Angeles, Arch R. Dooley of Harvard University, Daniel M. Holland of the Massachusetts Institute of Technology, Robert J. Holloway of the University of Minnesota, Donald P. Jacobs of Northwestern University, Bernard Karsh of the University of Illinois, Walter G. Kell of the University of Michigan, E. W. Martin, Jr. of Indiana University, and Joseph W. Newman of Stanford University.

With the publication of these latest winners, the Doctoral Dissertation Competition has completed its planned five-year span. My colleagues and I wish to express our appreciation for the generous assistance which the Ford Foundation has received from many people: Faculty members too numerous to mention have read and screened the more than 250 dissertations which have been submitted during the life of the competition, and Prentice-Hall has contributed its services to the publicizing and publishing of the selected dissertations.

CLARENCE H. FAUST
VICE PRESIDENT
THE FORD FOUNDATION

New York, N.Y.
January, 1964

Acknowledgments

The writer is particularly indebted to Dr. Thomas G. Andrews, under whose direction the study was conducted. Dr. Andrews contributed liberally of his time during the course of the study. His wise counsel and coordinative efforts greatly diminished the problems inherent in conducting the study away from the Maryland campus.

The following faculty members read the manuscript and made helpful suggestions: Dr. Nancy Anderson, Dr. Claude Bartlett, and Dr. Matthew Yarczower. Additionally, Dr. Allen Solem and Dr. Charles Cofer were of assistance in the early stages of the study.

Dr. Glenn Wilcox and Dr. Vincent Calia were of extensive assistance in obtaining subjects for the study at Boston University.

Mr. Richard Levitan, announcer for the training tapes, contributed many evening hours cutting the tapes at the studio facilities of Station WSRO in Marlboro, Massachusetts.

The Education, Marketing and Management Foundation was of financial support through presenting the 1961 Psi Chi Research Award for the proposal of the study.

The writer also wishes to express a special note of thanks to Raytheon management for their endorsement of the study. More specifically, the encouragement of my supervisor, Dr. Henry R. Brenner, and his numerous comments on various drafts, are appreciated.

Finally, I wish to express gratitude to my wife Marlene and three children, Sandy, Beth, and Pam for their patience and understanding during the many hours spent on the study.

FORREST W. FRYER

Contents

CHAPTER 1

General Introduction

Goals and goal directed behavior are important constructs in motivational theory. Prior to the 1930's, however, little formal attempt had been made to study goals as phenomena in themselves. The effects on the behavior of the individual of attainment and nonattainment of goals were actively investigated during the next two decades. During that period, and since, the so-called "level of aspiration" became a popular topic of research activity for those interested in the experimental investigation of various aspects of goal-setting behavior.

The term "level of aspiration" was introduced into the literature in Germany by Dembo in 1930 in connection with a study of the dynamics of anger (Dembo, 1931). Utilizing Dembo's suggestion that the presence of a particular "level of aspiration" determined whether or not the subjects felt satisfied or dissatisfied with themselves after performance on a task, Hoppe (1930) investigated the concept in an empirical study. This work reflected a certain degree of informality, with conclusions based upon the subjects' spontaneous remarks concerning their reactions to the various situations, the manner in which they worked at the tasks, and their statements relative to success and failure. In essence, the subjects' implicit level of aspiration was inferred chiefly on the basis of whether the performance appeared to be followed by feelings of success or failure.

Five years later, Frank (1935a) reported a quantitative technique for the experimental study of level of aspiration which became the standard technique in the field. This technique was anticipated in some respects by Hausmann (1933). In Frank's technique, the subject was informed of his performance score from the preceding trial and was asked to indicate "how well he intended to do" on the next trial. Thus an explicit level of aspiration was operationally defined as "the level of future perform-ance in a familiar task which an individual... explicitly undertakes to reach" (Frank, 1935a, p. 119). Further, it was assumed that reaching this goal constituted success, and not reaching it failure. With this defi-nition it was possible to obtain discrepancy scores among the following four points of a typical sequence in the level of aspiration situation:

1. last performance,
2. setting of level of aspiration for the next performance,
3. new performance,
4. the psychological reaction to the new performance.

Two popular discrepancy scores were the differences between the level of the last performance (1) and the level of the new goal (2) (called *goal discrepancy*) and the difference between the goal level (2) and that of the new performance (3) (called *attainment discrepancy*). Both the direc-tion and the size of the attainment discrepancy were seen as two of the major factors affecting statements of success or failure.

Most of the subsequent research in the area of level of aspiration was concerned with an analysis of the sources, the tension-systems, or the needs from which the level of aspiration develops. Pertinent reviews include an elaborate theoretical article by Lewin, Dembo, Festinger, and Sears (1944), as well as methodological reviews by Rotter (1942a) and by Ricciuti (1951). However, subsequent research on the problem of the level of aspiration can also be viewed as falling into two other distinct groups—namely, diagnostic and success prediction. The diagnostic cate-gory is represented by the attempts to use level of aspiration in describing stutterers (Lerea, 1954; Mast, 1952; Sheehan and Zelen, 1955), deaf children (Rutledge, 1954), delinquents (Stevens, 1952), and peptic ulcer patients (Hecht, 1952). Then too, similar attempts have been directed to the study of behavior patterns of neurotics (Himmelweit, 1947), schizophrenics (Jost, 1955), extraverts–introverts (Pierce, 1954), mal-adjusted children (Escalona, 1948), as well as general cultural compari-sons (Boyd, 1952; Bruner and Rotter, 1953; Sinha, 1955). The success prediction category of level of aspiration studies is represented by Heller (1952), who predicted success in a training program in a hosiery oper-ation, and by Klein (1948), who predicted success in flight training by the use of level of aspiration.

A variety of tasks have been utilized in the level of aspiration studies. These include psychomotor tasks (such as dart throwing, card sorting, quoit throwing), manipulation tasks, manual skill development tasks, cognitive tasks (verbal and nonverbal), athletic participation, and college examinations. Most of the studies tend to be laboratory rather than applied research, this constituting one of the limitations in the research literature on level of aspiration. Furthermore, most of the studies have employed level of aspiration as a dependent, rather than an independent variable.

Training has long been, and continues to be, a key area of activity in industrial psychology. Yet there has been relatively little in the literature on level of aspiration which can be directly utilized in industrial training, skill development, and related activities. Over the years, psychological research has isolated a number of principles of learning felt to be important and manipulatable factors in the training situations of industry and the military (McGehee, 1958; Wolfle, 1946, 1951). However, a primary orientation in an industrial training situation would be to incorporate a principle such as level of aspiration into the training process in order to manipulate behavior rather than use the concept as an analytical tool for analysis of past behavior. Therefore, the training value of level of aspiration is the locus of interest rather than a trial-by-trial analysis of the aspiration scores for investigating the process itself. Since the typical industrial training situation involves knowledge of results, it is important to determine whether level of aspiration (consisting of knowledge of results plus setting of a goal) possesses a motivational property, as reflected in total performance, beyond that of knowledge of results alone. Also, using level of aspiration as a training procedure may reflect a differential sensitivity to the various difficulty levels of a task. Finally, the instructional variables of goal-setting may have an influence on performance. It is with these hypotheses that the present study is concerned.

Review of Pertinent Literature

Even though the determinants of level of aspiration have been a popular source of experimental investigation, this section will review only selected studies in the area. The choice of studies under the major headings which follow was made on the basis of relevance to the present study.

Initial Setting of the Level of Aspiration. Lewin (1944) reported that most subjects, when first exposed to a level of aspiration

situation, set an initial level of aspiration higher than the previous performance score (defined as a positive goal discrepancy) and tend to keep
it positive under most conditions. Gould (1939) supported both conten-
tions made by Lewin.

Success or Failure. Many studies have centered on this particular
aspect, and general support is given to Lewin's (1944) contention that
success and failure directly affect the level of aspiration. The majority
of studies reveal that the level of aspiration is raised and lowered in
accordance with the attained or unattained level of aspiration represented by the preceding performance.

Gardner (1940) found that if the performance equals the level of
aspiration, the level of aspiration is likely to swing upward. Conversely,
an unattained desired level of performance leads to lowering the level of
aspiration.

Klugman (1948) observed that subjects who failed half or more times
to attain their level of aspiration on the Rotter Aspiration Board tended
to have lower goal discrepancy scores than those subjects who succeeded
more than half the time.

Child and Whitney (1949) reported that success generally led to
raising of the level of aspiration, whereas failure had the opposite effect.
Further, the greater the degree of success, the more likely the infla-
tion of the level of aspiration. The effects of failure were more varied
than were the effects of success.

Jucknat (1937) demonstrated the effects of success or failure *within
a series* of ten mazes, one series solvable and the other nonsolvable. In
the solvable series, the level of aspiration was raised during the experiment, whereas in the nonsolvable series the level of aspiration fell.
Studies by Festinger (1942), Anderson and Brandt (1939), and McGehee
(1940) also support Jucknat's conclusions.

Bayton and White (1950) studied success-failure sequences using
contrived scores on the Minnesota Rate of Manipulation Test. It was
found that goal discrepancies were much lower for subjects experiencing
success-following-failure than for subjects experiencing failure-following-
success. Actual performance was better for those subjects working under
initial success rather than initial failure.

Steisel and Cohen (1951) studied two different degrees of failure and
found that both mild and severe successive failure had a deflating effect
upon the level of aspiration set by the subjects. An immediate reaction
to severe failure was a significant increase in actual speed of performance,
and this effect became more pronounced with successive failure.

There have been only several studies indicating that success experience does not raise the level of aspiration. Hilgard, Sait, and Margaret (1940) concluded that successful subjects are more cautious in goal-setting than unsuccessful subjects. The successful subjects tended to set goals at a lower level with succeeding performances, while unsuccessful subjects persisted in estimations of improved scores. Further, the point was made that, despite the lowered level of aspiration with successful performances, these subjects continued to perform in a superior manner unlike the unsuccessful persons.

Pennington (1940), studying the effects of passing or failing grades in the classroom, found that success did not produce marked upswings in the level of aspiration. However, it was found that failure in the examination deflated subsequent levels of aspiration and that this tendency toward lower levels of aspiration was greater with numerous failures.

Although several studies are not in clear support of the statement, the majority of reviewed studies indicate that the level of aspiration will generally be raised and lowered as performance attains or does not attain the level of aspiration.

Transfer of Level of Aspiration. Jucknat's (1937) study discussed previously also demonstrates the extent to which a transfer effect within the same activity can take place. Those subjects who first attempted the solvable mazes set higher levels of aspiration than those who initially attempted the nonsolvable mazes.

Simon, Shaw, and Gilchrist (1954) also explored this transfer effect in a study utilizing a modified bowling game with a curtain hiding the target, thus facilitating the reporting of false performance scores. The prearranged performance scores were of four types: an increasing series of scores, a decreasing series, a combination of first increasing and then decreasing series of scores, and finally a combination of first decreasing and then increasing series. The subjects assigned to the latter two types of prearranged scores showed a latency effect after the initial scoring series was reversed. For instance, the increased level of aspiration associated with the increasing series of scores continued well into the trials of decreasing series of scores *before* the drop in level of aspiration took place.

Frank (1935c) utilized a task of normal difficulty, followed by one which was considered hard for one group and one which was considered easy for another group. His finding was that the initial height of the level of aspiration was higher when the normal task was followed by an easy task than when the task was followed by a hard task.

Instructional Variations of Expect versus Hope. Lewin (1944) originally referred to a continuum of reality-irreality upon which the level of aspiration is found. An unrealistic attitude—that is, out of contact with the preceding performance—was seen to result in a large goal discrepancy score and a more rigid level of aspiration, both of which would be reflective of the wishful thinking accompanying goal-setting. On the other hand, a realistic attitude was seen to result in a small goal discrepancy score with a level of aspiration that would be both flexible and responsive to change in performance.

Both Dembo (1931) and Hoppe (1930) in their initial studies of level of aspiration defined the concept with clear reference to the *goals* or *hopes* of the individual, but later work has frequently departed from this definition and has instead invoked *expectations* or *predictions*. An example of an estimate of future performance in terms of goals would be "What will you try to do?" By contrast, a statement in terms of expectations would be "What do you expect to do?"

Irwin (1944) has pointed out that level of aspiration involves both cognitive and affective factors and prefers to use level of expectation, except in cases where goals are *clearly* implied. Irwin distinguished between realistic and unrealistic aspirations in terms of expectations and goals. Realistic aspirations were viewed as those aspirations based upon an appraisal of the extent to which the individual is capable of meeting the demands of the situation with which he is confronted. In this respect, realistic aspirations were seen as evoked by "expect" instructions. On the other hand, unrealistic aspirations were viewed as those aspirations which are based upon the hopes, fears, and wishes originating in the individual—and evoked more directly by "hope" instructions.

Irwin and Mintzer (1942) demonstrated the effect that instructional variables have on levels of aspiration. A group exposed to "hope" instruction for stating the aspiration level was compared to a group given "expect" instruction. The mean goal discrepancy score of the "hope" group was significantly larger than the mean goal discrepancy score of the "expect" group. The instructional variables also resulted in two other differences in goal-setting behavior. The "expect" group had twice as many negative goal discrepancy scores as the "hope" group, and to a significant degree changed their aspiration level from trial to trial more frequently than the "hope" group.

Preston, Spiers, and Trasoff (1947), using dart throwing as a task, studied the effect of "hope" versus "expect" instructions as well as various difficulty levels and incentive conditions. The levels of aspiration for the "hope" group were significantly higher (at the 0.01 level) than those of the "expect" group. Although the study did not utilize any statistical controls for initial ability in dart throwing, the performance scores revealed an interesting interaction with amount of preliminary practice given. The performance scores of the "expect" group tended to be higher than the "hope" group in the minimum practice condition (10 trials), while the "hope" group tended to have higher performance scores than the "expect" group under extensive practice (50 trials). These differences were not statistically significant, however, and no statistical controls for initial ability were exercised.

Preston and Bayton (1942) systematically compared three levels of aspirations: (1) Maximum Level—the score which the subject feels represents his ultimate ability (using "hope" instruction), (2) Actual Level—the score which the subject expects to make on the next trial, estimated as accurately as possible (using "expect" instruction), and (3) Least Level—the score below which the subject is certain he will not fall. All three instructions elicited different levels of aspiration, with a very substantial correlation between Maximum and Actual Levels, but the Least Level had a low correlation with the other two. In brief, there was a tendency to place Actual Levels closer to Maximum than to Least Levels. Utilizing three dissimilar tasks, MacIntosh (1942) has confirmed this relationship.

Ricciuti and Schultz (1953), in developing group testing techniques for measuring level of aspiration, contrasted "expect" and "goal" instructions and found that the latter instructions produced a somewhat greater range of individual differences.

Holt (1946), asking some subjects for expectations and others for goals in a college course examination situation, found that the discrepancy scores for "goal" instructions were significantly larger than the discrepancy scores for "expect" instructions.

Another indication of the importance of particular instructions is reflected by Sears' (1940) experiment in which improvement in performance over a sequence of trials was dependent upon the degree to which the subjects set realistic goals. Horwitz, Exline, Goldman, and Lee (1953) also suggested that when goals are unrealistically established, the directive effect of goal-setting is lacking and improvement in the task will come more slowly. In essence, this handicap is a joint function of losing contact with the "realities" of the learning situation and the impression that overall improvements appear far short of the goal after initial unattainability in the early trials.

Further indication that unrealistic goals (striving for perfect performance at once) are less effective than realistic goals (involving gradual and stepwise increments in level of aspiration) is presented by Lockette (1956). Having high school students work on the manual skill task of planing wooden blocks to pre-set dimensions, he found that students using realistic goals clearly performed more effectively than those using unrealistic goals. An additional finding of particular importance to the present study was that the improvement in performance scores took place during the first part of the session, with the last third of the session only maintaining, rather than increasing the degree of improvement.

Yacorzynski's (1941) study reported that an unrealistically high level of aspiration was not related to heightened motivation or incentive, and achievement. A more realistic level of aspiration was, however, related to those factors.

In summarizing the effectiveness of "expect" versus "hope" instructions, no clear pattern is apparent. The study of Preston, Spiers, and Trasoff (1947) reflects an interaction with preliminary practice. "Expect" instructions have been shown to be superior (in terms of subsequent performance) in the studies of Horwitz et al. (1953), Lockette (1956), Sears (1940), and Yacorzynski (1941). It is possible that a factor underlying the conflicting findings has been the extent to which the instruction is emphasized and reiterated throughout a study. Lockette (1956), for instance, verbally verified the type of instruction by repeated references to examples between trials. Most of the other studies merely asked the subjects for their expectation or hope, with little or no clarification of what the instructions meant.

The instructional variable of "hope" versus "expect" would seem to be an important methodological consideration. While an individual's expectations are influential in determining what goals he will strive toward, it is also true that there are many expectations which do not coincide with goals at all. In asking for expectations rather than goals, the subject is presented with a clearly defined task, and hence uniformity of interpretation is presumably enhanced. On the other hand, asking for expectations is accomplished at the expense of failing to elicit much potentially valuable goal striving behavior. While it is true that tendencies to exaggerate or depreciate one's potentialities can be reflected in stated expectations or predictions of performance, it is probable that such estimations sample a much smaller portion of the dynamic characteristics involved in goal-striving behavior than is the case with estimations stated in terms of goals or hopes.

Ego-Involvement. The effects of ego-involvement on level of aspiration have been investigated in several studies.

Frank (1935c) indicated that ego-involvement in a task may arouse in the individual a desire to do well, leading him to set his level of aspiration too high. But on the other hand, Frank also indicated that ego-involvement might arouse a fear of failing, causing the individual to set his level of aspiration too cautiously, perhaps below his level of performance.

Harvey and Sherif (1951) found that estimating performances on an objective task showed no significant effects if two subjects are strongly ego-involved in a positive way. If competition, however friendly, existed, small discrepancies appeared in the estimation of the future performances of both competitors. However, if two subjects were antagonistically involved, wide and significant discrepancies were noted both in setting goals and in estimating future performances.

The effect of other people upon the level of aspiration was explored in a study by Rosenthal and Cofer (1948) where a group level of aspiration was obtained. Here, a deliberately indifferent and neglectful attitude by one member of the group resulted in a significant decrease both in belief in goal attainability and in belief that other group members would wholeheartedly participate to achieve the goal. Furthermore, there was a parallel decrease in ease of agreement in setting the group level of aspiration through discussion. Both individual and group levels of aspiration were similarly affected by success and failure.

Reference Groups. Another area of study in level of aspiration has been the influence of subjects being told the level of aspiration estimates and/or performances of various reference groups.

Festinger (1942), studying undergraduates working on synonym lists and information tests, explored the effects of three different reference groups on estimates of level of aspiration. In addition to being told his score after each trial, each undergraduate was also told the average level of aspiration and average performance of one of three groups—either high school students, college freshmen, or graduate students—before making his own estimate for the subsequent trial. In general, the undergraduates raised their estimates when told they were scoring below the reference group (especially for the high school reference group), and they lowered their estimates when scoring above a group (particularly the reference group of graduate students). Thus, there was a tendency to conform to the estimation level of the reference group. Furthermore, a contrast of "expect" and "hope" instructions in this study showed that the variability of goal discrepancy scores was lower under expect instructions.

Hertzman and Festinger (1940) found that when subjects were told the aspirations and the performances of their *own group*, the general trend was to change subsequent estimates of level of aspiration in the direction of the group's estimate. The majority of subjects shifted their explicit goals from their own previous estimates to those of the group estimates. It is of some interest to note that the investigators also found slight (but not statistically significant) improvements in second-half performance after the group estimates and performances had been made known during the first half of the study. However, their experimental design does not allow the possibility of determining whether this trend was a practice effect or the result of added information about the group.

MacIntosh (1942) studied the effects hypothetical scores of Negroes had on levels of aspiration of Caucasions. The subjects tended to raise the Actual and Maximum Levels and to hold the Least Level constant when they were told they were doing as well as Negroes (the converse of what Preston and Bayton had found when Negroes were told they were doing as well as Caucasions). This social variable was present in the cancellation and addition tasks, but not in the symbols-digits task.

Anderson and Brandt (1939) exposed a class of fifth grade school children to different cancellation tests for six times over a three-week period. Before the second testing session, the experimental group was told both their own score on the previous test as well as the average score for the entire class. The control group merely took the tests with no knowledge of their own scores or the scores of the class. The class had been separated previously into high and low achievers—the high achievers being more advanced in age and school work. The low achievers set goals considerably above their own achievement, and the high achievers did the reverse. Irrespective of the achievement level, however, the goals of the children tended to *converge* on what represented mediocrity for the group. In this study also, the experimental group performed significantly better than the control group, with the control group showing decreases in mean performance scores after the first test. However, the actual advantage of goal-setting is not readily determined in this study since the control group did not have knowledge of their own previous results before each testing session.

In a more recent study, Kausler (1959) studied the effect of reference group performance scores. Three groups of subjects performed on a simple arithmetic test under the three following conditions: Group C—without instructions to express a level of aspiration; Group L—with instructions to express a level of aspiration; Group LR—similar to Group L but with the additional information of a reference score (the average performance achieved by Group L). The reference score increased the level of expressed aspirations, since the level of aspiration group means were significantly higher, at the 0.05 level, for Group LR than Group L. The performance means for Group L were significantly higher than Group C at the 0.01 level. The performance means for Group LR were also significantly higher than Group C at the 0.01 level, but not significantly different from the performance means for Group L. Although expressing the level of aspiration served to increase the performance level on the subsequent task, the increase in level of aspiration between Group L and Group LR was not followed by a concomitant increase in performance. Since this study has direct implications for the present study, some of the problems in generalizing the results of Kausler's investigation will be treated in detail in a later section of this chapter.

Conditions of Expressing the Level of Aspiration. Studies in level of aspiration occasionally vary in terms of the conditions under which the level of aspiration is solicited. In some cases the subject verbally reports his estimate to the experimenter in an individual testing situation. In other cases, he announces the level of estimate in front of a group, while in still other studies the subject might record it on an identified or unidentified paper.

Several investigators have highlighted the implicit dangers in varying the conditions of expressing the level of aspiration. Gardner (1940) cautioned that the level of aspiration obtained in studies is no more than what the individual is willing to make public concerning his aims. He further emphasized that the public indication of what the subject aims to achieve may be true or false in terms of his actual aims. Holt (1944) differentiated between private goals (covert) and public goals (overt and sometimes different from the private goals). The subtlety of expressing level of aspiration is also reflected in a study by Hanawalt, Hamilton, and Morris (1943) where nonleaders in an academic situation later reported having higher private goals which they did not report during the experiment itself.

Mischel (1958) demonstrated that the public-private nature of the situation in which expectancy statements are elicited can significantly affect the subsequent modifiability of such statements. The subjects, following failure, were offered another opportunity to try the task. Subjects were found more likely to lower their estimates of their next scores if the first estimate had been private than if it had been public. Under both private and public conditions, the subjects wrote their estimates on a paper. However, the public condition was a direct, face-to-face relationship with the experimenter who saw the estimates written in an individual testing situation. The private condition was testing of groups in which the subjects, ranging in number from 5 to 15, were seated at desks widely separated from each other and the experimenter. It was found, to a statistically significant degree, that estimates of levels of aspiration were more resistant to change when the subject was in direct, face-to-face contact with the experimenter *or* when the subject inferred that the experimenter could view his performance.

Margaret (1942) reported a study in which subjects were exposed to a condition of private recording of performances and goals (written on a paper seen only by the experimenter) and another condition of posting both performances and goals in full view to a group of four. The tasks were quoit tossing and dart throwing. The effect of active participation in the social group was to alter the discrepancy scores so that they more nearly matched the reported group performance.

The methodological importance of the commitment aspects of the situation in which the subject sets his goal is also demonstrated by Armstrong (1947) in a study of performance as a function of expressed and nonexpressed levels of aspiration. Armstrong felt that a public level of aspiration statement would result in a greater need to succeed, since failure could mean ego deflation, loss of status, and loss of prestige in the opinion of another person. Four groups, performing on the Minnesota Rate of Manipulation Test, were established as follows: Group 1—no knowledge of results, no level of aspiration obtained; Group 2—knowledge of fictitious results, no level of aspiration obtained; Group 3—knowledge of fictitious results, set levels of aspiration but did not report them to experimenter; Group 4—knowledge of fictitious results, subjects verbally reported aspirations to experimenter. The results indicated that, for the first half of the total performance, the rank order for rate of improvement was Group 4, 3, 2, and 1. The only significant differences (at the 0.05 level) were those between Groups 4 and 1, and Groups 3 and 1. For the last half of the total performance, however, the differences between the Groups were not significant. The association between expression of aspirations and increasing levels of performance is an extremely interesting finding, since it demonstrates the impact that a methodological variation has on performance. However, a counteracting influence is the perhaps injudicious use of fictitious knowledge of results with this particular manipulation task. This problem will be treated in more detail in a later section of this chapter.

Difficulty of Task. In several studies, subjects were asked to indicate their levels of aspiration, not by making statements regarding future performance but by selecting for each trial the level of difficulty at which they wished to perform. Escalona (1948), for example, arranged twelve jig-saw puzzles in order of difficulty and, after each trial was completed, asked her young subjects to select the particular puzzle on which they wished to work for the following trial. Thus the level of the choice in each case was considered the level of aspiration. Escalona found that "overtly maladjusted" children lowered their level of aspiration less frequently after "controlled" failure than did the "overtly well-adjusted" children. Yacorzynski (1941) used the selection of less difficult methods of completing the task as a means of inferring a minimum degree of effort. Thus his conclusion was that performance scores had a tendency to be higher for the subjects putting forth the least effort (paralleled also by those having the higher aspirations).

However, exposing the subject to a range of difficulty in tasks and then noting performance change has not been extensively investigated. The study by Frank (1935c), mentioned in a previous section, is an exception. However, there the intent was to note shifts in the levels of aspiration rather than performance scores. The study by Preston, Spiers, and Trasoff (1947) utilized four difficulty levels but only found that hopes tend to increase as difficulty increases.

Sutcliffe (1955) studied level of aspiration as a function of task variability. Level of aspiration was found more dependent upon performance in a low variability task situation in which there is a clear indication of what will occur than in a high variability task situation which is more ambiguous. In the high variability situation, success produced optimism and elevated the level of aspiration while failure produced pessimism and depressed the level of aspiration.

Related Industrial Study. French (1950) has reported an industrial application of goal setting. Girls working on a sewing operation filled out pacing cards indicating the hours of the day during which they wanted to work at slow, medium, or fast paces. Although the stated decision involved not performance expectations but rather "speed of work" expectations, the concept of stating a goal is important for purposes of the present study. French found that varying the speed of work in accordance with their preferences had a beneficial effect on worker productivity and attitudes.

Summary of Literature. Several points would seem apparent from the preceding literature review. It can be seen that general problems in level of aspiration have been attacked with the use of varied tasks. Such problems include the initial setting of the level of aspiration, the effects of success or failure on level of aspiration, the transfer effect of level of aspiration, the instructional variations of "expect" versus "hope", the effects of ego-involvement and reference groups, the conditions under which the level of aspiration is expressed, and the difficulty of the task.

However, the number of applied studies directly concerned with *performance* changes have been relatively few in number. Further, systematic evaluations, when attempted, have had some shortcomings. For instance, Lockette (1956) generalized in his manual skill study that "goal-setting, either realistic or unrealistic, is superior to no goal-setting at all." This generalization must be viewed with reservation since his experimental comparison of the effects of goal-setting was to a "control" group which in essence exercised no control. The control group received sketchy instructions, was not even told of the elaborate scoring system for evaluating the planed blocks, and, of course, received no knowledge of results. The attitude of the control group is well reflected in the fact that they used only 85% of the allocated time available for work. This was in marked contrast to the goal-setting groups who were still working when the time limit was reached. Also, the scoring system was deliberately modified to keep scores from getting too high early in the experiment, as well as to give the groups the possibility of experiencing failure. However, the failure to contrast level of aspiration performance against a baseline of knowledge of results is most damaging. His study, in fact, does not indicate whether sheer knowledge of results or the goal-setting aspect of level of aspiration, or both, accounted for the enhanced performance.

In Kausler's study (1959) involving the arithmetic test, knowledge of results also was a crucial factor. His subjects had to state a level of aspiration in the absence of firm knowledge of results. The practice test, upon which the level of aspiration estimate was based, was rigidly timed and the typical subject completed less than half of the problems. The practice problems were not scored, and the subject presumably had to *infer* how accurately he had answered those practice problems completed and on this basis state how many problems he hoped to be able to answer *correctly* during the test period. Furthermore, the results by Kausler are limited only to a situation using "hope" instructions and working at a task of one difficulty level.

On the other hand, Armstrong's study (1947) reveals a comparison of expressed and nonexpressed levels of aspiration against a baseline of knowledge of results; however, the knowledge of results (on the Minnesota Rate of Manipulation Test) were fictitious and are suspect. Although a uniform series of fictitious performance scores does have the advantage of standardizing the reported level of performance and the shape of the learning curve for all subjects, there is an explicit disadvantage entailed in this procedure. Under such arrangements, certain tasks are of questionable appropriateness, since the subject's true level of performance must not be obvious to him. There is always the possibility that a subject may sense changes in his performance which appear to be contradicted by the scores reported to him, resulting in skepticism concerning the reported information. Evidence that this is a real problem has been reported by MacIntosh (1942). Certainly it would seem that reporting the subject's actual performance to him and asking him to set his aspiration level within that framework would make for a much more realistic situation.

Statement of the Problem

Skills can be defined in terms of well-adapted performance of varying kinds which are usually developed over a period of time through repetition and imitation. The establishing and developing of a variety of skills constitutes the domain of much industrial training. Although some psychological principles of importance have been isolated (Wolfle, 1951), the incorporation or "programming in" of these principles into the training procedure for the purpose of manipulating behavior remains a problem. The level of aspiration procedure represents a combination of the principle of knowledge of results with the additional element of goal-setting. Although the typical industrial training situation involves knowledge of results, the question remains as to whether the additional component of goal-setting in a skill development situation may, in fact, enhance performance. Three laboratory studies have been cited which to varying degrees represent attempts in this direction. However, the tasks have been of limited value and the experimental designs have been inadequate.

The present study, within the context of a skill acquisition task of learning to receive International Morse Code, will be concerned with the following specific questions:

1. Does the procedure of level of aspiration, consisting of knowledge of results plus goal-setting, possess a motivational property (as reflected in task *performance*) above that of knowledge of results *alone*?

2. Is this procedure of level of aspiration differentially effective with training tasks of varying difficulty levels?

3. Do the instructional variations of soliciting "expectations" compared to "hopes" differentially influence subsequent performance?

4. Does the method of expressing the level of aspiration, private or public, influence subsequent performance?

The experimental *hypotheses* of this study are as follows:

1. The mean performance scores of the group exposed to the procedure of level of aspiration will be significantly greater than the group having knowledge of results alone.

2. The procedures of level of aspiration and knowledge of results will have differential effects on tasks of high and low difficulty.

3. The mean performance scores of the group receiving the "expectation" instructions will be significantly different from the mean performance scores of the group receiving the "hope" instructions.

4. Public expression of level of aspiration, regardless of its exact nature, will significantly enhance mean performance over that of private expression of level of aspiration.

CHAPTER 2

Method and Procedure

The Task. The task for this study consisted of acquisition of skill in receiving International Morse Code, a special language developed from combinations of short and long sounds. This special language has been extensively used by the military and in some civilian groups for rapid transmission of messages. There have been at least four systematic reviews of the literature on code learning; and each review details the nature and uses of International Morse Code (Kurtz, 1959; Taylor, 1943; West, 1955; Windle, Sidman, and Keller, 1953).

The code-voice method of instruction was used for the code learning. This method was first described in the literature by Keller (1943), and is essentially a modification of the techniques of "paired associates" and "regular reinforcement." Basically, it consists of presenting a Morse Code signal, having the trainee make a response, telling the trainee the correct answer, and having him record the correct answer if his first response was wrong.

There were several reasons why code learning was selected as the task for this study. First, since the learning of International Morse Code is a type of skill training utilized in both peace and wartime, it represents a realistic and practical area of further exploration. Next, code learning is a type of task to which few college students have been previously exposed. This aspect, coupled with a method of screening out those few students who have had experience with International Morse Code, makes it possible to present a new learning situation to available trainees. Third, the code-voice instructional procedure easily lends itself to incorporation of the experimental variables of knowledge of results and goal-setting. Finally, the linear shape of the learning curve for this task permits a sensitive investigation of the effects of the experimental treatments upon performance during learning.

Concerning the last point on the shape of the learning curve, recent research has not confirmed the learning plateaus noted in the classic studies of Bryan and Harter (1897; 1899). Instead, recent studies usually find learning curves with such slight negative acceleration that the curves do not differ markedly from linearity (Air Ministry Training Research, 1946; Keller, 1958; Keller, 1959; Kurtz, 1959).

Experimental Design. The study used a 2 × 2 × 2 factorial design (with two fractionated groups for knowledge of results) as shown in Table 1. This design permits a direct determination of three main effects as well as the various interactions. The main effects are the following:

1. Type of Instruction—whether the level of aspiration is solicited in terms of "expect" or "hope" instructions. The key questions eventually established were:

   "The score I *expect* to make on this trial is _____,"

   and

   "The score I *hope* to make on this trial is _____."

TABLE 1. THE TEN EXPERIMENTAL GROUPS OF THE STUDY

	Low Difficulty Code Characters	High Difficulty Code Characters
Expect Instruction	A Private Expression B Public Expression	C Private Expression D Public Expression
Hope Instruction	E Private Expression F Public Expression	G Private Expression H Public Expression
Knowledge of Results Alone	I	J

2. Method of Expressing the Level of Aspiration—whether the level of aspiration is a "private" or "public" expression. As indicated in Chapter 1, the literature varies in terms of what constitutes a privately expressed level of aspiration. For purposes of this study, however, a "private" expression of level of aspiration is one in which the estimate is confidentially recorded by the trainee on his booklet without verbal announcement of the estimate. "Public" expression of level of aspiration refers to the condition in which the trainee exposes his written level of aspiration to the other trainees in the group by announcing it aloud to the proctor so that the level of aspiration can be recorded next to the trainee's seat number on a blackboard display.

3. Difficulty of the Material—whether the code letters are of "low" difficulty or "high" difficulty. "Low" difficulty code letters are those letters subject to less frequent errors during learning by previous trainees.

Furthermore, the design makes it possible to compare the effects of "Knowledge of Results Alone"[a] to "Level of Aspiration" for each of the two difficulty levels.

Dependent Variables. Five dependent variables were selected as criteria to reflect performance. Four of the five criteria were scores over arbitrarily selected blocks of training trials, consisting of signals presented in random order. The criteria were:

1. The total number of correct responses in trials 4, 5, 6, and 7 of the training session (hereafter referred to as Block 1).

2. The total number of correct responses in trials 8, 9, 10, and 11 of the training session (hereafter referred to as Block 2).

3. The total number of correct responses in trials 12, 13, 14, and 15 of the training session (hereafter referred to as Block 3).

4. The total number of correct responses for the last ten trials of the training session, trials 6 through 15 (hereafter referred to as Block 4).

5. The number of correct responses on a code test after completion of the training session of fifteen training trials.

---

[a] In this study "Knowledge of Results Alone" involved no solicited level of aspiration. Although the trainees under this condition were not given instructions to set a level of aspiration, it is always possible that some trainees may have personally set a level of aspiration.

The advantage of Block 4 as a criterion is that it yields a comparison of effects for the major portion of the training session rather than the usual comparison made with terminal scores, such as the fifth criterion, or with fractionated portions of the training session, such as the first three criteria (Kogan, 1954). The first three criteria, on the other hand, make it possible to determine the "phasing" of the effects of level of aspiration through stages of skill development. For instance, some of the studies cited in the literature review indicated that the initial effect of level of aspiration was not always sustained throughout the entire session (Armstrong, 1947; Lockette, 1956). Through a comparison of Blocks 1, 2, and 3 in the present study, it is possible to determine whether any initial effect is increasing or decreasing through the rest of the training session.

Pretests. Four pretests were made before the main study. These pretests were conducted with two different subject groups; the first two pretests occurred in the Fall and Spring semesters of 1958–1959 and used undergraduate students in the laboratory section of a course in experimental psychology at the University of Maryland. The last two pretests were conducted during the Fall semester of 1959 and utilized undergraduate students in a course in guidance at the College of Industrial Technology at Boston University.

Pretest 1. The purposes of this initial pretest were to establish the timing of the Morse Code signals and to develop the basic, standardized instructions for the study. Two learning tapes, containing machine-cut signals for uniform sound, were obtained from the U. S. Army Southeastern Signal School. Each signal was sent at a speed which, if the standard interval between successive signals were maintained, would approximate a rate of eighteen to twenty words per minute. This transmission rate is considered as standard rate for beginners in Morse Code (Kurtz, 1959, p. 5). The pretest established that this rate was not inappropriate for the college students. Also an optimal inter-signal interval of four seconds was used. Furthermore, the Army instructions were modified and made more specific to the student group.

Pretest 2. Next, the particular Morse Code letters for the study were selected and the high and low difficulty levels of the letters were confirmed. Additionally, an estimate of the reliability of the code test (the fifth criterion) was obtained.

The relative order of difficulty of alphabet code letters had been independently established in two different studies (Keller and Taubman, 1943; Spragg, 1943). The correlation between the rank orders was +0.91; however, the rank orders had been established on the basis of learning the entire alphabet. Since a maximum contrast of difficulty levels was required, the order of difficulty of the code letters in the above-mentioned studies could not be accepted. It was therefore necessary to derive two distinct groups of code letters, differing in difficulty level.

Two groups of nine letters each were selected from the Spragg study, which based order of difficulty upon a composite difficulty index of errors of omission (no response to the signal) and errors of substitution (incorrect response to the signal). The nine high difficulty letters thus isolated were, in order of decreasing difficulty, W, P, Y, X, Q, J, F, L, and U. The nine low difficulty letters, in order of increasing difficulty, were E, T, I, M, N, H, A, B, and R. Three low difficulty letters from the Spragg study which were deliberately screened out prior to the pretest were V, S, and O, since it was felt that there was some possibility the trainees would have had prior experience with these familiar and popular signals.

Twelve students were utilized in this second pretest, with the students equally divided between the high and low difficulty code groups. The groups were exposed to fifteen training trials, with each trial consisting of twenty-five signals presented in random order. Upon conclusion of the training trials, a test of forty-five signals (again the nine signals in random order) was administered. The results of the test are presented in Table 2.

TABLE 2. COMPARISON OF AVERAGE TEST SCORES FOR THE LOW AND HIGH DIFFICULTY GROUPS IN PRETEST 2

Code Letter Group	No. of Students in Each Group	Average Test Score (No. of Signals Correct out of Possible 45)	t-test Value	t-test Value for 0.05 Level of Confidence with 10 df
High difficulty	6	18.17	1.983	1.812
Low difficulty	6	33.67		

It can be seen from Table 2 that the overall difference of 15.50 was significant at the 0.05 level (one-tailed test). Thus the two difficulty levels of the code letters were confirmed for purposes of the present study.

In addition, the reliability of the forty-five signal test was also determined. The reliability was estimated from item homogeneity and makes the assumption only that the average covariance among nonparallel items is equal to the average covariance among parallel items (Gulliksen, 1950, p. 224). The reliability for the test was high, with a value of 0.97 for the high difficulty test and 0.96 for the low difficulty test. It was thus concluded that the code tests were reliable measures of code learning performance, and the next pretest was initiated.

Pretest 3. At this point, two groups of subjects were available for one hour at Boston University; and a contrast of "hope" versus "expect" instructions was attempted, using the high difficulty code letters. Although the groups only had time to work through six of the fifteen training trials, two important results were apparent. First, the "hope" group had a larger average goal discrepancy between performance and level of aspiration than did the "expect" group. Thus the subjects in the "hope" group were setting a relatively higher level of aspiration than the subjects in the "expect" group. Second, the "hope" group had made slightly better progress during the limited training session. However, the actual performance of the two groups had varied to such an extent that the pretest seemed an inadequate test of instructional differences.

Pretest 4. Another group of sixteen students was located at Boston University for Pretest 4. This same pretest served as a final run for an activity check list to screen out those students who had prior exposure to International Morse Code. All students received a test booklet which summarized the intent of the study and asked them for their cooperation in imagining they were participating as a student in the study. The written entries gave trial-by-trial scores for the various training trials to all students. The fact that the scores were identical for all students was not made known to them. The students were merely asked, given the indicated performance on the prior training trial, to set a level of aspiration for the next trial. The following instructional conditions were examined in the four separate groups:

1. The score I *hope* to make on this trial is _____.
2. The score I *optimistically hope* to make on this trial is _____.

3. The score I *realistically expect* to make on this trial is _____.
4. The score I *expect* to make on this trial is _____.

The intent was to determine whether the instructions for the middle two conditions were adding any clarity in goal-setting and whether the slight differential in goal discrepancy scores from Pretest 3 would be verified. The fictitious scores written on separate pages of the test booklet represented an average score of 12.6 letters correct out of 25 possible, based on average performance on the same high difficulty letters in Pretest 2. The results from Pretest 4 are found in Tables 3 and 4.

TABLE 3. ANALYSIS OF VARIANCE OF AVERAGE GOAL DISCREPANCY SCORES OF THE FOUR GROUPS IN PRETEST 4

Source	SS	df	MS	F	$F_{0.05}$
Between groups	56.455	3	18.818	5.280	3.490
Within groups	42.762	12	3.564	—	—
Total	99.217	15			

An examination of Table 3 indicates that there was significant "Between Group" variation in the average goal discrepancies for the four groups in Pretest 4. Furthermore, Bartlett's test for homogeneity of variance (Lindquist, 1953) revealed a chi square value which was not significant ($\chi^2 = 6.735$, $df = 3$, $p > 0.05$), thus indicating homogeneous variances. The four groups were then compared to each other and the results are found in Table 4.

It can be seen that the average goal discrepancy was largest under the "hope" instruction and smallest under the "expect" instruction. The difference between the two discrepancies (using a two-tailed test) was statistically significant at the 0.01 level of confidence, thus indicating the two instructions had different effects. Since a contrast of the distance of the goal beyond the level of past performance was important to the study, the two instructional variables of "hope" and "expect" were used in the main study which will now be discussed.

Conduct of the Main Study. It was imperative that all of the experimental groups, within each of the two difficulty levels, receive

TABLE 4. COMPARISON OF AVERAGE GOAL DISCREPANCY SCORES FOR THE
FOUR GROUPS OF PRETEST 4 EXPOSED TO DIFFERENT INSTRUCTIONS CON-
CERNING THE SETTING OF THE LEVEL OF ASPIRATION

Instruction For Level of Aspiration	No. of Students in Each Group	Average Goal Discrepancy	Groups Compared	df	t-test Value
(1) Hope	5	5.369	(1) vs (2) (1) vs (3) (1) vs (4)	7 5 8	0.884 2.474 3.595**
(2) Optimistically Hope	4	4.250	(2) vs (3) (2) vs (4)	4 7	1.705 2.506*
(3) Realistically Expect	2	1.462	(3) vs (4)	5	0.235
(4) Expect	5	1.077	—	—	—

Throughout the study,

    * A single asterisk will be used to indicate
    significance at the 0.05 level of confidence.
   ** A double asterisk will be used to indicate
    significance at the 0.01 level of confidence.
 *** A triple asterisk will be used to indicate
    significance at the 0.001 level of confidence.

identical Morse Code signals. This was accomplished by machine cutting the group of high and low difficulty code letters and then reproduc-
ing ten individual tapes for the ten experimental groups. The only difference among the tapes was in the verbal instructions.

The trainees for the study consisted of one hundred male freshmen
and sophomores from the College of Industrial Technology and the
Junior College at Boston University. The trainees were students in a
required weekly course on guidance given during the Fall and Spring
semesters of 1959–1960. All ten classes, numbering from thirteen to
twenty-five students, agreed to participate in the study and were asked
to fill out the activity check list previously mentioned as a portion of
the fourth pretest (an example of the check list is given in Appendix A).
The check list had been designed to identify those students who had
prior experience with International Morse Code. Any student who indicated on the activity check list that he had participated in the activities
of "Ham Radio Operator," "Morse Code Reception," or "Signal Flag

Activities" was excused from the study. Simultaneously, any excess beyond ten trainees for each group also was excused. In reducing the classes down to ten trainees each, those students who had marked the activities of "Armed Forces" and "Boy Scouts" were also screened out when possible, since there was some possibility that such individuals might have retained some memory of Morse Code signals from such service and scout activities. It might also be pointed out that all trainees possessed normal auditory acuity as determined by a college entrance physical examination. Finally, each class of ten trainees was randomly assigned to one of the ten treatment conditions in the experimental design.[b]

Procedure for the Training Session. The tape recorder, located in front of the numbered chairs, was in position before the trainees entered the test room. The chairs were arranged in two rows of five chairs each. The trainees sat in the numbered chair of their own choosing. After all ten trainees were seated, the tape recorder was turned on and the tape, containing the entire instructions for the training session, was played.

The complete text of all ten training tapes is given in Appendix B. However, a summary of the instructions will be discussed at this point to give a general overview of the study. The study was presented as a comparison of training techniques in the learning of International Morse Code. International Morse Code itself was explained as well as the use of the phonetic alphabet. The trainees were informed that their task would be to learn nine specific code letters, and the training booklets on their seats were explained. They were then introduced to the sound of the nine code letters (preceded by the phonetic name of each letter) with each signal repeated five times for emphasis. This served as an introduction to the signals as well as initial practice in responding every time they heard a signal. This procedure was repeated a second time for the nine code letters.

Next, the first signal was sounded singly without the phonetic name. At this point, the various ways of responding were treated in detail by examples. Each sheet in the training booklet consisted of a series of double rows of five squares. The *top* row of each block of squares was to be used to indicate the trainee's initial identification of the signal.

---

[b] Random assignment on a group basis is not, of course, the best way to achieve a true randomization. However, since the subjects were available only during class time, the random assignment had to be made on a group basis.

The bottom row was to be used only if the trainee found that his initial response was in error (as determined by the announcer on the tape naming the signal three seconds after the signal was sent). The point was made that the response system allowed each trainee to score his paper quickly after each training trial.

The trainees were informed that a test to measure their learning of the code letters would be given at the end of the training session, and that the test would not include the identification of each signal by its phonetic name. The trainees were given two reasons for encouragement in anticipating the identification of the signal by responding on the top row of response squares *before* the announcer named the signal: first, a proctor would be monitoring the group; and secondly, failure to antici-pate the signal during the training trials would not prepare them for the final test.

The practice period continued with the sounding of each of the nine signals. The same signals were then sounded in reverse order, and the trainees were told that the fifteen training trials would begin. In addition, they were informed that each trial would contain twenty-five signals, with the nine code letters appearing in a random order.

All ten groups received identical instructions for the first two train-ing trials. After both trials, the trainees counted the number of entries on the bottom row, subtracted this from twenty-five, and entered the number of correctly identified signals in a space marked "Score" at the bottom of each sheet.

After the second training trial had been scored, the remaining trials differed for the ten treatment conditions. This difference involved the procedures occurring between successive trials. The trainees under the two Knowledge of Results (KOR) conditions were asked to tally their number of correct responses (out of a maximum of twenty-five), record the score on the sheet, and move on to the next trial. The trainees under the remaining eight treatment conditions, however, were (after scoring) all asked to set a level of aspiration for the next trial. Those trainees in the "expect" condition were asked to set a goal by filling in the following statement on the top of the sheet for the new trial:

"The score I *expect* to make on this trial is _____."

Trainees under the "hope" conditions were asked to set a goal by filling in the following statement:

"The score I *hope* to make on this trial is _____."

Verbal elaboration on the key words of "expect" and "hope" was given to the trainees. For the "private" condition, no further information on the indicated level of aspiration was solicited. However, under the "public" condition, each trainee was asked to announce aloud his written level of aspiration to the proctor so that it could be recorded next to the trainee's seat number on a blackboard display. Furthermore, the order of presenting levels of aspiration was systematically rotated by seat number to give each trainee an opportunity to respond first.

After the seventh training trial, all trainees in the study were given a five-minute rest period. During the rest period, the trainees were required to maintain silence and to remain seated. After the completion of the fifteenth training trial, a test of forty-five signals (with no verbal identification) was presented. Finally, the trainees were thanked for their cooperation in the study, and the necessity of their not discussing the study with anyone was emphasized.

CHAPTER 3

Results

The basic data of the study are given in Appendix C. The data are presented in complete detail for each of the ten experimental groups, with trial-by-trial scores for individual trainees.

Since analysis of covariance was the basic statistical approach used in the study, the assumptions which should be fulfilled to properly use the analysis of covariance technique will first be discussed. Detailed discussions of analysis of covariance can be found in most statistical texts, such as those of Lindquist (1953) and McNemar (1955).

Basic Assumptions in the Study. The assumptions of analysis of covariance are that:

1. The population of observations is normally distributed.
2. The treatment cells are assigned randomly.
3. The treatment effects are constant and additive.
4. The variances are homogeneous.
5. The regressions are homogeneous.

The first two assumptions are handled through experimental design whereas the last three assumptions are checked by statistical calculations. The first assumption is clarified by a determination of the population at which the investigation is being directed and by selection of a normal sample from that population. This was done in the present study by defining the trainee group and selecting college students as sufficiently typical of the trainee group. The second assumption was adequately fulfilled by the experimental procedure of assigning the trainee groups to the ten treatment cells in a random fashion.

As mentioned previously, a statistical confirmation is possible for the last three assumptions in the analysis of covariance procedure. The Bartlett test (Lindquist, 1953) was used for checking the third and fourth assumptions, and a homogeneity of regression solution was computed to verify the fifth assumption.

The 0.05 level of significance was selected for this study. However, to present all the information that has been obtained, higher levels of significance will be reported wherever appropriate. The step-by-step sequence of an analysis of covariance solution will be discussed in some detail in the first analysis of the main study data so that the presentation of subsequent analyses can be expedited.

Comparison of Average Goal Discrepancies. The first question asked of the data in the main study was whether the "expect" and "hope" instructions resulted in the setting of different goal levels. It will be recalled that Pretest 4 had revealed a statistically significant difference between the average goal discrepancies for the two instructions. The first analysis in the main study, then, was to assure that the two types of instructions were continuing in their effect in the main study.

The assumption of homogeneous variances was checked by the Bartlett test. This test for homogeneity of variance of the average goal discrepancies revealed a significant chi-square value ($\chi^2 = 40.312, df = 7$, $p < 0.001$). Since the average goal discrepancy scores did not satisfy the assumption of homogeneous variances, a logarithmic transformation (after adding a constant of 4.0 to each goal discrepancy score) was applied. With this transformation the data fulfilled the homogeneity of variance requirement ($\chi^2 = 13.523, df = 7, p > 0.05$). Furthermore, the treatment effects could be considered constant and additive on the responses of the trainees in the sample on which the treatment was imposed. Thus another covariance assumption was fulfilled.

Having checked the homogeneity of within-group variance, the next requirement was to determine the F-value of the between-group variance since one can proceed to a more detailed analysis of specific treatment effects only if the between-group variance is significant. This analysis is presented in Table 5.

An examination of Table 5 indicates a significant overall between-group treatment effect for the transformed average goal discrepancies. However, the initial performance level for the individual trainees could very well have varied widely; and not taking this into account could lead to misleading results. Therefore, an analysis of covariance control (McNemar, 1955) was utilized. The covariance procedure is a statistical

TABLE 5. ANALYSIS OF UNADJUSTED Y (LOGARITHMIC TRANSFORMED
AVERAGE GOAL DISCREPANCY SCORES)

Source	SS	df	MS	F	$F_{0.001}$
Between groups	0.982596	7	0.140371	12.615	4.37
Within groups	0.801166	72	0.011127	—	—
Total	1.783762	79			

TABLE 6. ANALYSIS OF THE SIGNIFICANCE OF REGRESSION OF LOGARITHMIC
TRANSFORMED AVERAGE GOAL DISCREPANCY SCORES ON THE SUMMATION OF
THE TWO INITIAL TRAINING TRIALS

Source	SS	df	MS	F	$F_{0.01}$
Reduction due to Regression	0.101039	1	0.101039	10.246	7.08
Residuals	0.700127	71	0.009861	—	—
Total (within groups)	0.801166	72			

technique for adjusting criterion scores with respect to some control
variable. In this study the control variable was the summation of the
first two training trials of each trainee. Thus the transformed average
goal discrepancy scores were adjusted in terms of their regression on the
two initial training trial scores. In this way, any differences in adjusted
goal discrepancies could be attributed to the experimental treatments
beyond the first two trials since in essence each trainee's baseline of
performance on the first two trials has been taken into consideration.

To evaluate the advantage of analysis of covariance in the present
study, it was necessary to determine whether any efficiency was introduced by the covariance technique. This was achieved by determining
the significance of regression of the transformed average goal discrepancies on the control variable. The results of that analysis are found in
Table 6.

The results of Table 6 indicate that the assumption of a real correlation between the goal discrepancies and control variable is justified.
Another way of indicating the increase in precision attributable to covariance adjustment is to determine the percentage drop in error variance. For example, the original error variance for unadjusted goal discrepancies was shown to be 0.011127 in Table 5. When that part of the
error variance attributable to initial scores was removed, the error variance for adjusted goal discrepancies in Table 6 became 0.009861. This

represents an increase in precision of 12 percent, or a 12 percent drop in error variance.

For the last covariance assumption involving homogeneity of regression, the errors of estimation from the average regression were determined. Table 7 containing that analysis indicates the F-ratio is not significant. Consequently the assumption of homogeneous regression is justified for the data.

Having established the extent to which the goal discrepancy data satisfied the assumptions of analysis of covariance, the next step was the analysis of covariance itself, which is presented in Table 8.

TABLE 7. ANALYSIS OF THE HOMOGENEITY OF REGRESSION OF LOGARITHMIC TRANSFORMED AVERAGE GOAL DISCREPANCY SCORES ON THE SUMMATION OF THE TWO INITIAL TRAINING TRIALS

Source	SS	df	MS	F	$F_{0.05}$
Deviations from individual group regressions	0.631510	64	0.009867	—	—
Differences among group regressions	0.068617	7	0.009802	0.993	2.25
Total deviations from the average regression within group	0.700127	71			

TABLE 8. ANALYSIS OF COVARIANCE OF THE LOGARITHMIC TRANSFORMED AVERAGE GOAL DISCREPANCY SCORES

Source	SS	df	MS	F
Instruction (A)	0.600107	1	0.600107	60.857***
Expression (B)	0.000236	1	0.000236	0.024
Difficulty (C)	0.306561	1	0.306561	31.088***
AB	0.007573	1	0.007573	0.768
AC	0.003591	1	0.003591	0.364
BC	0.090700	1	0.090700	9.198**
ABC	0.009912	1	0.009912	1.005
Error	0.700127	71	0.009861	—
Total	1.718807	78		

** Significant at 0.01 level of confidence.
*** Significant at 0.001 level of confidence.

An inspection of Table 8 reveals that two of the three main treatment effects were significant, both at the 0.001 level. The Instruction effect indicates a significant difference in goal discrepancies between the groups receiving "expect" instructions and the groups receiving "hope" instruction. Adjusted means, computed by taking into account the trainees performance on the first two trials, were 0.62218 for the "expect" group and 0.79613 for the "hope" group. The significant difficulty effect demonstrates that the groups exposed to high difficulty code characters had lower goal discrepancies (adjusted mean = 0.61441) than the groups exposed to low difficulty code characters (adjusted mean = 0.80389). Said another way, the goal level of the high difficulty groups was significantly more conservative than the goal level of the low difficulty groups. The failure of the expression effect to reach significance shows that the public compared to the private expression of the level of aspiration had no substantial effect on goal discrepancies. The interaction of expression and difficulty (BC) was significant at the 0.01 level and it was the only significant interaction effect. Table 9 demonstrates this significant interaction effect, using adjusted means reflecting the trainees' performance on the first two trials.

The specific nature of the interaction between expression and difficulty can be readily seen in Table 9. The average goal discrepancy of the public expression group was *higher* than the average goal discrepancy of the private expression group for the low difficulty code characters (0.84001 compared to 0.76778) but was *lower* than the private expression group for the high difficulty code characters (0.58175 compared to 0.64707). Thus the interaction can be defined in terms of the failure of the public expression group to have consistently higher goal discrepancies than the private expression group for the two difficulty levels. Note also

TABLE 9. ADJUSTED MEANS OF THE LOGARITHMIC TRANSFORMED AVERAGE GOAL DISCREPANCY SCORES FOR THE EIGHT EXPERIMENTAL GROUPS, CLASSIFIED BY EXPRESSION AND DIFFICULTY

	Private Expression of Level of Aspiration	Public Expression of Level of Aspiration	Means
Low difficulty code characters	0.76778	0.84001	0.80390
High difficulty code characters	0.64707	0.58175	0.61441
Means	0.70743	0.71088	—

the extent to which the marginal means for the difficulty effect differ considerably (reflecting the significant main effect) while the marginal means for the expression effect are almost identical (indicative of the expression main effect that was not significant).

In summary, the highlight of the comparison of average goal discrepancies in the main study was that the expect instruction solicited a smaller (and statistically significant) average goal discrepancy than the "hope" instruction. It could thus be concluded that the two instructions had different effects for the trainees in the main study.

Relationships Between the Five Criteria. Five criteria were initially selected as measures of learning performance; however, it was necessary to determine the degree of inter-relationship between the criteria before proceeding with the analysis. The fact that four of the five criteria represented scores over selected blocks of training trials increased the importance of such an analysis. The intercorrelation matrix of the five criteria is shown in Table 10.

It can be seen from Table 10 that the intercorrelations are all positive, and that the five criteria are highly related to each other. In fact, the *lowest* intercorrelation is 0.809. Because of the high intercorrelations, the average correlation of each criteria was computed, using the z transformation technique (McNemar, 1955, p. 148), in order to select the one criterion for emphasis in the analysis. Table 10 indicates that the highest average correlation was associated with Block 4. Block 4, by representing the summation of scores on training trials 6 through 15 (thus actually encompassing part of Block 1 and all of Blocks 2 and 3),

TABLE 10. ZERO ORDER INTERCORRELATIONS OF THE FIVE CRITERIA FOR THE 100 TRAINEES AND THE AVERAGE CORRELATION OF EACH CRITERION

	Block 1	Block 2	Block 3	Block 4	Test Score
Block 1 (sum trials 4 → 7)	1.000	0.915	0.888	0.939	0.809
Block 2 (sum trials 8 → 11)	—	1.000	0.941	0.984	0.843
Block 3 (sum trials 12 → 15)	—	—	1.000	0.980	0.876
Block 4 (sum trials 6 → 15)	—	—	—	1.000	0.873
Test score	—	—	—	—	1.000
Average correlation of each criterion	0.897	0.941	0.936	0.961	0.852

was also logically the most appropriate criterion to emphasize. Therefore, the subsequent analyses of the data will emphasize the Block 4 criterion by using Block 4 as the sole criterion for hypothesis testing, and the other four criteria will be included only as background information.

Level of Aspiration versus Knowledge of Results Alone.
The first two hypotheses of the study involved the role of knowledge of results and how it differs from level of aspiration. To determine whether level of aspiration has a motivational characteristic above or beyond that of knowledge of results alone, the performance scores of the groups exposed to level of aspiration procedures were pooled and contrasted to the performance scores of the groups exposed to knowledge of results alone for the combined difficulty levels. Table 11 summarizes the analysis.

In Table 11 it can be seen that the Block 4 criterion (the summation of trials 6 through 15) had a significant F-value (at the 0.05 level). Although the other criteria are presented only as background information, it is of some interest to note the failure of Block 2 and the Test Score to reach significance. It should be emphasized here that the experimental procedure contained two occurrences, immediately prior to the beginning of the Block 2 and the Test Score criteria, which may have importance.

TABLE 11. COMPARISON OF SCORES BETWEEN THE KNOWLEDGE OF RESULTS (KOR) GROUP ($N = 20$) AND THE LEVEL OF ASPIRATION (LOA) POOLED GROUP ($N = 80$) FOR THE COMBINED DIFFICULTY LEVELS

Criterion	F $df = 1/97$	Adjusted Means KOR	Adjusted Means LOA	t-test Value $df = 98$
Block 1 (sum trials 4 → 7)	5.579*	41.75	50.45	3.821***
Block 2 (sum trials 8 → 11)	2.764	47.58	56.10	—
Block 3 (sum trials 12 → 15)	5.678*	50.61	62.15	3.239**
Block 4 (sum trials 6 → 15)	4.888*	119.92	144.64	3.270**
Test score	0.026	23.84	25.62	—

* Significant at 0.05 level of confidence.
** Significant at 0.01 level of confidence.
*** Significant at 0.001 level of confidence.

These occurrences were a five minute rest period given to all groups after the completion of trial 7, and the test instructions given to all groups after the completion of trial 15. Although the implications of the rest period will be discussed in a later section, it might be mentioned here that the five minutes of silence, in addition to permitting rest, may have offered an opportunity for the trainee's experimental set to be disrupted.

Adjusted means were computed to determine which group had better performance scores, taking into account the initial performance on the first two training trials. In Table 11, the adjusted means for the three criteria which had the significant *F*-values indicate that the level of aspiration group performed better than the knowledge of results group. More specifically, the difference between the two groups for the Block 4 criterion was significant at the 0.01 level (using a one-tailed test of significance). Although the *F*-values for the Block 2 and test score criteria were not significant, the adjusted means for those criteria were also computed to determine whether the level of aspiration group continued to be superior, even though not at a statistically significant level. Table 11 indicates that such was the case.

At this point, then, Hypothesis 1 had been tested, using Block 4 as the single criterion. The null hypothesis was rejected and the specific hypothesis was accepted that:

> The mean performance scores of the group exposed to the procedure of level of aspiration will be significantly greater than the group having knowledge of results alone.

TABLE 12. COMPARISON OF SCORES BETWEEN THE KNOWLEDGE OF RESULTS (KOR) GROUP ($N = 10$) AND THE LEVEL OF ASPIRATION (LOA) POOLED GROUP ($N = 40$) FOR THE LOW DIFFICULTY CODE CHARACTERS.

Criterion	F $df = 1/47$	Adjusted Means	
		KOR	LOA
Block 1	0.307	62.72	64.42
Block 2	0.762	66.96	71.22
Block 3	2.374	69.69	76.82
Block 4	0.086	169.00	181.00
Test score	1.274	33.74	32.99

The next analysis involved the extent to which the procedures of level of aspiration and knowledge of results alone produced different results for the two *separate* difficulty levels in the study. Table 12 summarizes the analysis for the low difficulty code characters and Table 13 contains the analysis of the high difficulty code characters.

An examination of Table 12 reveals that none of the F-values were significant and it was concluded that for the low difficulty code characters, there was no significant difference in performance between the knowledge of results group and the level of aspiration pooled group. However, it might be noted that for the Block 4 criterion, as well as three of the remaining four criteria, the adjusted mean of the level of aspiration group was higher. Nevertheless there were no statistically significant differences in this analysis of low difficulty code characters.

Table 13, however, indicates a quite different situation for the high difficulty code characters. All criteria except the test score showed a significant F-value and their respective t-test values were significant, with the t-test value of Block 4 being significant at the 0.05 level (two-tailed test). The pattern was one where the level of aspiration group was significantly superior in performance on each criterion, except the test score. By a contrast of the Block 4 criterion in Tables 12 and 13, Hypothesis 2 had been tested. Here also the null hypothesis was rejected and the specific hypothesis was accepted that:

The procedures of level of aspiration and knowledge of results will have differential effects on tasks of high and low difficulty.

TABLE 13. COMPARISON OF SCORES BETWEEN THE KNOWLEDGE OF RESULTS (KOR) GROUP ($N = 10$) AND THE LEVEL OF ASPIRATION (LOA) POOLED GROUP ($N = 40$) FOR THE HIGH DIFFICULTY CODE CHARACTERS

Criterion	F $df = 1/47$	Adjusted Means		t-test Value $df = 48$
		KOR	LOA	
Block 1	10.632**	26.80	36.63	3.263**
Block 2	4.828*	32.99	41.41	2.198*
Block 3	5.799*	35.65	47.96	2.408*
Block 4	6.888*	82.81	109.14	2.623*
Test score	1.024	15.63	18.56	—

* Significant at 0.05 level of confidence.
** Significant at 0.01 level of confidence.

In brief, for *high* difficulty code characters, level of aspiration was more effective in improving performance scores than was knowledge of results alone.

Comparison of Expect versus Hope Instruction and Private versus Public Expression of the Level of Aspiration. The last two hypotheses of the study involved the extent to which different instructions and different manners of expressing the level of aspiration affect the learning performance. To expedite the discussion, the following tables, indicating the extent to which the assumptions of covariance were fulfilled for the performance scores, have been placed in the Appendix:

Appendix D. The data for all five criteria fulfilled the homogeneity of variance requirement.

Appendix E. There were significant overall between-group treatment effects for the five criteria.

Appendix F. The significance of regression analysis indicated the efficiency of the covariance control.

Appendix G. The regressions were homogeneous for all five criteria.

The analysis of covariance for Block 4 is shown in Table 14.

An inspection of Table 14 reveals that difficulty was the only main treatment that was significant (at the 0.01 level). Since a basic portion of the experimental design was a contrast of high and low difficulty code characters, it was of course expected that gross differences in difficulty would occur. The failure of the instruction effect to reach significance

TABLE 14. ANALYSIS OF COVARIANCE OF THE BLOCK 4 CRITERION (SUMMATED PERFORMANCE SCORES ON TRAINING TRIALS 6 THROUGH 15)

Source	SS	df	MS	F
Instruction (A)	2,556.11	1	2,556.11	3.32
Expression (B)	44.79	1	44.79	0.06
Difficulty (C)	7,543.57	1	7,543.57	9.79**
AB	1,613.75	1	1,613.75	2.09
AC	1,283.68	1	1,283.68	1.67
BC	210.37	1	210.37	0.27
ABC	933.45	1	933.45	1.21
Error	54,719.26	71	770.69	—
Total	68,904.98	78		

** Significant at 0.01 level of confidence.

shows that *expect* instructions, compared to "hope" instructions, had no substantial effect on performance scores. Also, the expression effect indicates no significant differences between the performance scores of those publicly and privately expressing their level of aspiration. In short, neither the instructions given for the level of aspiration nor the manner of expressing the level of aspiration had any substantial effect on performance scores. The fact that the first order and second order interactions did not reach significance demonstrates that the various interactions of the three treatment effects had no substantial influence on performance scores.

As background information, the analysis of covariance tables for the other four criteria are listed in Appendix H. An inspection of Appendix H indicates essentially the same results—that is, the difficulty treatment effect was *consistently* significant for all criteria. However, it can be seen in Appendix H that the instruction treatment effect was significant early in the training session (Block 1, representing trials 4 through 7). To determine the direction of that instruction significance for Block 1, as well as to determine the direction of the effects (though not statistically significant) in the remaining four criteria, the unadjusted and adjusted treatment means were computed. Table 15 summarizes that analysis.

Table 15 reveals that the "hope" group had a better performance on the first criterion (an average adjusted score of 54.16 compared to 48.94 for the "expect" group). The mean difference of 5.22 was significant at the 0.01 level. Furthermore, the "hope" group in the last four criteria had a higher adjusted mean, although caution must be exercised due to lack of statistical significance of the last four criteria.

TABLE 15. COMPARISON OF SCORES BETWEEN THE EXPECT INSTRUCTION GROUP ($N = 40$) AND THE HOPE INSTRUCTION GROUP ($N = 40$) FOR THE FIVE CRITERIA

Criterion	Unadjusted Means		Adjusted Means	
	Expect	Hope	Expect	Hope
Block 1	50.02	53.08	48.94	54.16
Block 2	56.25	58.10	55.22	59.13
Block 3	61.32	65.00	60.38	65.94
Block 4	143.35	151.08	140.87	153.58
Test score	24.92	27.30	24.48	27.74

TABLE 16. COMPARISON OF SCORES BETWEEN THE PUBLIC EXPRESSION GROUP ($N = 40$) AND THE PRIVATE EXPRESSION GROUP ($N = 40$) FOR THE FIVE CRITERIA

Criterion	Unadjusted Means		Adjusted Means	
	Public	Private	Public	Private
Block 1	53.90	49.20	52.84	50.26
Block 2	57.52	56.82	56.50	57.84
Block 3	62.40	63.92	61.46	64.86
Block 4	148.28	146.15	145.81	148.62
Test score	25.85	26.38	25.41	26.82

A study of Table 15 also reveals the effect of the covariance adjustment. Although the "hope" group had a lower score than the "expect" group in the first two training trials (19.15 compared to 20.35), Table 15 indicates that the "hope" group had a *higher* score on the first criterion. This is reflected in the contrast of the unadjusted and adjusted means, with the "hope" group increasing from an unadjusted mean of 53.08 to an adjusted mean of 54.16. At the same time the "expect" group dropped from an unadjusted mean of 50.02 to an adjusted mean of 48.94.

Although the expression treatment effect was not significant for any of the criteria, the adjusted means for the public and private expression groups were also computed to determine the direction in scores. That analysis is presented in Table 16.

Table 16 indicates that the group expressing their level of aspiration publicly showed an advantage on only the first criterion, Block 1. From that point on, the private expression group showed an advantage, although again it is important to note that none of these differences were significant.

Thus, by the use of Block 4 as a criterion, it was possible to test Hypotheses 3 and 4 of the study. Neither null hypothesis could be rejected. Therefore, Hypothesis 3 which stated that:

> The mean performance scores of the group receiving the "expectation" instructions will be significantly different from the mean performance scores of the group receiving the "hope" instructions,

could not be accepted. On the same basis, Hypothesis 4 which stated that:

> Public expression of level of aspiration, regardless of its exact nature, will significantly enhance mean performance over that of private expression of level of aspiration,

could not be accepted.

A summary of the results is presented in Table 17 to give an overview of the study and to serve as a single reference for the discussion of results which follows.

TABLE 17. SUMMARY TABLE OF THE RESULTS OF THE STUDY, INDICATING THE FOUR EXPERIMENTAL HYPOTHESES AND WHETHER THE VARIOUS CRITERIA ALLOWED THE REJECTION OF THE NULL HYPOTHESES

Experimental Hypotheses of the Study		Block 1 Criterion	Block 2 Criterion	Block 3 Criterion	Block 4 Criterion	Test Score Criterion
Hypotheses 1 and 2 LOA > KOR	Combined Difficulty Levels	Reject Null	—	Reject Null	Reject Null	—
	Low Difficulty Levels	—	—	—	—	—
	High Difficulty Levels	Reject Null	Reject Null	Reject Null	Reject Null	—
Hypothesis 3 Expect ≠ Hope		Reject Null	—	—	—	—
Hypothesis 4 Public > Private		—	—	—	—	—

— indicates the null hypothesis was not rejected. Although Block 4 was the only criterion actually used for hypothesis testing, this table presents the results for each criterion to facilitate an overview and later discussion.

Discussion of Results

The demonstrated superiority of performance scores of the level of aspiration group over the knowledge of results group clarifies the advantage of goal-setting over knowledge of results alone. As discussed in Chapter 1, several previous studies (Armstrong, 1947; Kausler, 1959; Lockette, 1956) also had arrived at this conclusion. However, the experimental designs and/or procedures of those studies were of such a nature that acceptance of such a conclusion had to be considered tenuous. The present study for the task involved clearly demonstrates the superiority of goal-setting as measured by subsequent learning performance. Furthermore, this study has demonstrated that goal-setting can be readily incorporated into the training procedure itself, rather than remaining only as a trainer's concern which might be verbally imparted to trainees in a form such as "You should set a goal for yourself." In short, it moves a step beyond the level of "You should set a goal for yourself" to the point of "What is the goal you *have set?*"

The extent, however, to which this goal setting superiority is *not* consistent across the two difficulty levels points out the importance of the difficulty variable in studies of level of aspiration. That level of aspiration was significantly better than knowledge of results for high difficulty code characters but not significantly better for low difficulty characters indicates the extent to which the difficulty of the training material influences the advantage of level of aspiration as a training technique. Since level of aspiration as a training technique was not equally effective across difficulty level, there is added impetus for giving close attention to the selection of the task in a study on level of aspiration. Since task difficulty appears to have been generally ignored as a variable in previous studies, it is highly probable that some of the inconsistencies in the literature of level of aspiration could be clarified by closely examining the difficulty level of the task. This would appear to be the case since most of the tasks employed were of the routine, simple variety and since the present study indicates that the low end of the difficulty continuum is less sensitive to the procedure of level of aspiration than the high end of the difficulty continuum.

Even more importantly, the significant difficulty effect in the present study points to the selectivity which should be utilized in further efforts at using level of aspiration as a training procedure. Clearly, the implication from this study suggests that goal-setting is more beneficial as a training technique in material of high difficulty. Whether this advantage eventually reverses itself at even higher difficulty levels or for other types of materials or tasks is yet to be explored.

The failure of the instruction main effect ("hope" versus "expect") to have a more profound influence on performance is not easily interpreted. It is apparent from an inspection of the covariance tables in Appendix H that individual differences increased throughout the training trials. The climbing interactions from Block 1 to Block 3 most likely obscured the main effects. Although the "hope" instruction resulted in significantly superior performance for Block 1 (trials 4 through 7), its advantage over the "expect" instruction was not sustained in subsequent trials. Since the five minute rest interval took place immediately after the seventh training trial, there is reason to suppose that set dissipation may have taken place at that time. The rest period required silence and although the verbal instructions were designed to re-establish the set, it would appear that this was unsuccessful. It is of some interest to note that both Armstrong (1947) and Lockette (1956) also observed a first half effect. Both investigators reported that the results from the first half of the experiment were merely sustained rather than increased in the second half of the experiment. Thus there is some suggestion that dissipation of set is a particularly vulnerable aspect of studies in level of aspiration.

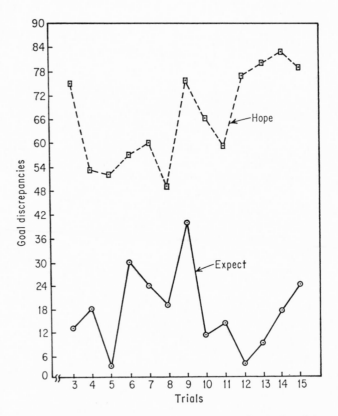

Fig. 1. Average goal discrepancy scores by individual training trials, contrasting the "hope" and "**expect**" instructions for the *low* difficulty level

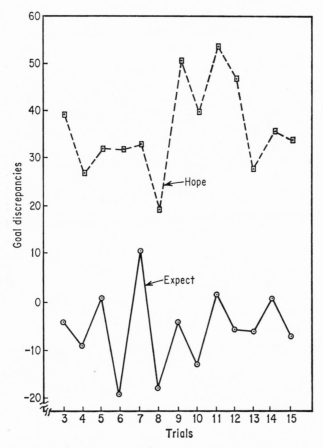

Fig. 2. Average goal discrepancy scores by individual training trials, contrasting the "hope" and "expect" instructions for the *high* difficulty level

Several definitive statements can be made, however, concerning what did *not* happen in the instruction main effect of the present study. First, the failure of the "hope" group to sustain their advantage in performance scores might have been explained had the average discrepancy scores fallen off markedly following trial 7. Although this was noted in the Kausler and Trapp (1958) study, such was not the case in the present study. Figure 1 for the low difficulty group and Figure 2 for the high difficulty group show that there was an immediate drop in average goal discrepancies after the seventh trial; however, this initial drop was quickly regained and the average goal discrepancies, on an overall basis, continued at an essentially steady or increasing level for the remainder

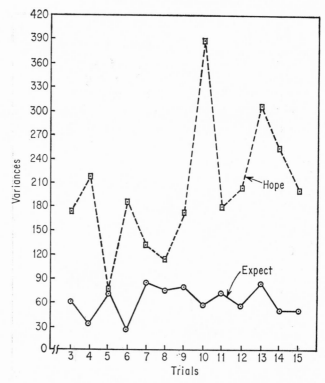

Fig. 3. Variances of average goal discrepancy scores by individual training trials, contrasting the "hope" and "expect" instructions for the *low* difficulty level.

of the training trials. Thus, a dropping of the goal discrepancy scores (evidenced by the setting of a relatively lower goal level) cannot be offered as an explanation for the "hope" group failing to sustain their initial performance level.

Second, the variability of the goal discrepancies of the "hope" group was not completely inconsistent with previous studies. As noted by Festiner (1942), the variance of the goal discrepancies of the "hope" group was somewhat higher than the variance of the "expect" group. This is depicted in Figs. 3 and 4. Figure 3 demonstrates that the variance of goal discrepancies for low difficulty code characters for each individual trial was higher under the "hope" instruction. Thus it can be seen that the discrepancy scores were changed more often than discrepancy scores of the "expect" group. This pattern is not as strong for the high difficulty code characters (Fig. 4) where the "hope" group had a higher variance of goal discrepancies in only nine of the thirteen trials.

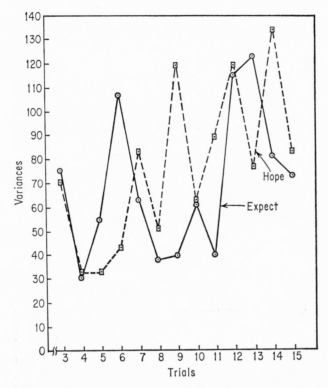

Fig. 4. Variances of average goal discrepancy scores by individual training trials, contrasting the "hope" and "expect" instructions for the *high* difficulty level

Third, the relationships of the negative goal discrepancies were not inconsistent with previous studies. When appearing in the present study, negative goal discrepancies occurred more frequently under the expect than "hope" instructions (Fig. 2), thus supporting the findings of Irwin and Mintzer (1942).

In substance then, it can be noted that the instruction main effect was generally neither an atypical nor a significant variable in the present study. It made little difference, as far as learning performance was concerned, whether "hope" or "expect" instructions were given since either instruction was superior to knowledge of results alone.

The lack of any significant differences resulting from the method of expressing the level of aspiration is more readily interpreted. As mentioned in the literature review, there have been varying operational definitions of the "public-private" dimension of expressing the level of aspiration. The present study was perhaps restricted by not selecting bipolar aspects of this continuum. The difference between the public and private expression was only in terms of whether the trainee verbally revealed his level of aspiration to the rest of the group. In both conditions, the estimate was eventually revealed as the trainee handed back his booklet to the proctor at the end of the experimental session. To this extent, indirect social pressure was present in the private condition as well, and it can be seen that the approach used in setting up the expression variable did not result in a maximum contrast. Furthermore, it is possible that revealing performance scores as well as the levels of aspiration would have had a greater motivational effect, perhaps resulting in a better performance by the public commitment group. Nevertheless, the public commitment did result in reducing the variability of the levels of aspiration, as shown in Figs. 5 and 6. Figure 5 for the low difficulty level indicates that the variance of the levels of aspiration of the public group dropped below the level of the private group after an initially higher level. A similar pattern is evident in Fig. 6 for the high difficulty level in that the variance of the levels of aspiration of the

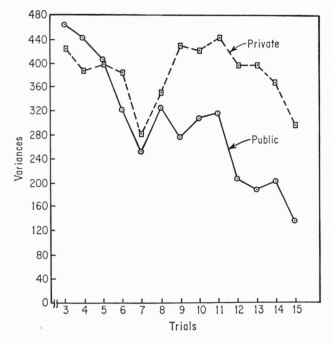

Fig. 5. Variances of levels of aspiration by individual training trials, contrasting the private and public expressions for the *low* difficulty level

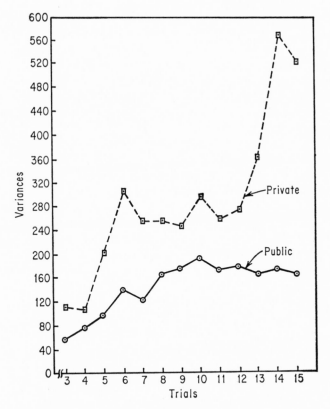

Fig. 6. Variances of levels of aspiration by individual training trials, contrasting the private and public expressions for the *high* difficulty level

public group was consistently lower than the variance of the private group. The results of the present study are in general agreement with the study by Mischel (1958).

Some discussion is warranted concerning the role of the test score criterion in Table 17. Had all criteria been used for hypothesis testing, it can be seen that the test score would have been the only criterion for which *all* null hypotheses would not have been rejected. The test differed from the training trials only in the number of test signals and, of course, of the correct identification of the signal by the announcer. Although it is possible that the trainees were responding during the training trials *after* the correct identification of the signal by the announcer, this explanation is not readily acceptable since the small groups were closely monitored by the proctor. It is possible, of course, that the mere change in procedure, represented by the witholding of knowledge of results, contaminated performance during the test. No formal reactions to the test itself were solicited or obtained, and so the results of the test score criterion are not readily understood. Any further research should certainly explore this phenomenon. However, the finding does emphasize the desirability of designing a study where intermediate, as well as final indices of performance are obtained. In short, *had* this study relied only on the single test score criterion, valuable intermediate occurrences would have been lost and completely negative findings would have prevailed.

It would appear obvious that there is a need for further investigation concerning the role of level of aspiration as a training procedure. This study has demonstrated that goal-setting results in significantly superior performance over knowledge of results alone. There is a strong suggestion that the training procedure is particularly beneficial with material of high difficulty. Further research should be directed toward a more intensive exploration of various degrees of high difficulty material. Unless there is a further interest in exploring the circumstances of the failure of the instruction and expression variables, such future research need not be particularly concerned with whether the instructions are given in terms of "expect" or "hope", or whether the manner of expressing the level of aspiration is public or private.

Another area of future research on level of aspiration as a training procedure might involve the manner and effectiveness of group goals set from the outside compared to individual personal goals. Increasingly, military and industrial organizations are finding it necessary to set goals, in training programs as well as numerous other activities. How to introduce these goals, in what manner, and at what expense could be an adjunct to a study in level of aspiration as a training technique.

A likely follow-up to the present study would be the removal of the five minute rest period to explore whether the apparent dissipation of set would still take place. There is an additional question as to the generalization of the findings of the present study. This study concerned itself only with the task of International Morse Code utilizing the code-voice method of instruction. To what other training techniques and/or training materials can these findings be generalized? This is the role of further research. One particular aspect of interest to the present investigator is the possible advantage of level of aspiration in a skill development task where the trainee must consider more than a single criterion of performance. For instance, does goal-setting result in better overall typing performance where the twin criteria of minimum errors *and* maximum speed are operating?

CHAPTER 4

Summary

This study has been concerned with an evaluation of level of aspiration as a training procedure. More specifically, an attempt was made to determine whether incorporating, or programming in, level of aspiration into the training procedure itself would enhance learning performance. Relatively few studies have treated level of aspiration as an independent variable. Furthermore, those studies which have differentiated between, and shown the superiority of, level of aspiration (consisting of knowledge of results plus setting of a goal) over knowledge of results alone, have used tasks of limited value and experimental designs and/or procedures of an inadequate nature.

The task for the study consisted of acquisition of skill in receiving International Morse Code, utilizing the code-voice method of instruction. Four pretests were necessary to clarify the instructions, the choice of code characters, and the experimental procedures. In the main study, one hundred male freshmen and sophomores from Boston University were assigned to the ten treatment cells of a $2 \times 2 \times 2$ factorial design (with two fractionated groups for knowledge of results). The three main treatment effects investigated by analysis of covariance were:

Type of Instruction—Soliciting the level of aspiration in terms of "expect" ("the score I *expect* to make on this trial is _____") or "hope" ("the score I *hope* to make on this trial is _____").

Method of Expressing the Level of Aspiration—expressing the level of aspiration in "private" (trainee confidentially recorded the level of aspiration on his booklet) or in "public" (trainee recorded the level of aspiration on his booklet and announced it to the proctor who displayed it on a board in front of the group).

Difficulty of Material—code characters of "high" or "low" difficulty, with difficulty referring to the number of errors made by previous trainees during the learning process.

Five dependent variables of learning performance were initially isolated, with four of the criteria representing scores on selected blocks of training trials. The fifth criterion was a code test after the completion of the training session of fifteen training trials.

The results of the main study indicated that the pretest finding concerning the size of the average goal discrepancies had been supported. After a logarithmic transformation to achieve homogeneous variances, it was found that two of the main treatment effects (instruction and difficulty) were significant at the 0.001 level, and one interaction (expression × difficulty) was significant at the 0.01 level. The groups receiving *expect* instruction had a smaller average goal discrepancy than the groups receiving the *hope* instruction, and likewise the groups exposed to high difficulty code characters had lower average goal discrepancies than the groups exposed to low difficulty characters.

The relationships between the five criteria were explored by computing zero order intercorrelations. All of the intercorrelations were high and positive. This necessitated the computation of the average correlation of each criterion (via the z transformation technique) to select one criterion for hypothesis testing and for emphasis in the analysis. Block 4, representing the summation of scores on training trials 6 through 15, was thus selected.

In an effort to determine whether level of aspiration has a motivational characteristic beyond that of knowledge of results alone, the performance scores of the groups exposed to level of aspiration procedures were pooled and contrasted to the scores of the knowledge of results group for the combined difficulty levels. The Block 4 criterion had an F-value which was significant at the 0.05 level. Mean scores were adjusted by taking into account the initial performance of each trainee on the first two training trials. The level of aspiration pooled group had a score significantly higher, at the 0.01 level, than the knowledge of results group. The clear advantage of level of aspiration was thus established and the first experimental hypothesis concerning the superiority of level of aspiration instructions was accepted.

The same analysis was then conducted on the two *separate* difficulty levels to explore whether level of aspiration and knowledge of results would have differential effects on high difficulty as contrasted to low difficulty material. For the low difficulty code characters, there was no significant difference; however, for the high difficulty characters, the level of aspiration group had significantly superior performance scores. This resulted in an acceptance of the second experimental hypothesis concerning the differential effects of the two techniques on material of differing difficulty.

The last two hypotheses involved the extent to which different instructions and differing manners of expressing the level of aspiration affect the learning performance. Although the instruction main effect was significant for the criterion involving the initial training trials 4 through 7, (with the "hope" group distinctly better than the "expect" group), this effect was not present in the Block 4 criterion used for hypothesis testing purposes. This finding was discussed by referring to an apparent dissipation of set during the five minute rest period immediately following the seventh training trial. The only significant main treatment effect for the Block 4 criterion was the difficulty effect, reflecting the basic design of the study. There were no significant differences between "expect" or "hope" instructions and between private or public expression of the level of aspiration, although there was a tendency for the "hope" instruction and private expression to have higher (but not significant) performance scores. On this basis, the last two experimental hypotheses concerning the differential effects of instruction and the superiority of public expression could not be accepted.

It was emphasized that the inconsistency of the superiority of goal setting across the two difficulty levels accentuates the import of difficulty as a variable in level of aspiration studies. This finding calls for closer attention to the selection of a task and implies that level of aspiration will have more training benefit in material of greater, rather than lesser, difficulty.

Although the failure of the instruction main effect is not readily understood, it was apparent that individual differences increased through the training session. There was confirmation of some previous studies, however, since the variance of the goal discrepancy scores was higher for the "hope" group than for the "expect" group, and negative goal discrepancies occurred less frequently in the "hope" group.

The lack of any significant difference between the groups who expressed their level of aspiration in private or in public was discussed in terms of the extent to which the two methods of expression were perhaps not of maximum contrast. In short, there was some indirect social pressure even in the private expression since the level of aspiration was eventually revealed to the proctor by the trainee handing back his booklet. Nevertheless, the public expression was associated with a lower variance of the levels of aspiration than was the case with the private expression.

Although this study for the task involved has demonstrated the superiority of goal setting, further research in several areas would appear warranted. More attention should be given to an exploration of the difficulty variable and the extent to which goal-setting continues to be beneficial as the higher limits of the difficulty variable are reached. The dissipation of set should be studied further to lengthen the apparent short-term benefit of the "hope" instructions. Finally, the appropriateness of level of aspiration as a training procedure for tasks which require attending to multiple criteria for effective performance should be examined. Clearly however, this study has implications for industrial training in that it has demonstrated that goal-setting readily and beneficially can be incorporated into the training procedure itself in the code-voice method of instruction of International Morse Code.

SELECTED BIBLIOGRAPHY

Air Ministry Training Research, *Hours of Work in Learning Morse. Report on an Experiment at Madley, April-Dec. 1945*. London, England: Air Ministry, Science **4**, 1946.

Anderson, H. H., and H. F. Brandt, "Study of Motivation Involving Self Announced Goals of 5th Grade Children and the Concept of Level of Aspiration," *J. Soc. Psychol.*, 1939, **10**, 209–232.

Armstrong, Doris E., "Performance as a Function of Expressed and Nonexpressed Levels of Aspiration," Unpublished master's thesis, Howard University, 1947.

Bayton, J. A., and E. Whyte, "Personality Dynamics During Success-Failure Sequences," *J. Abnorm. Soc. Psychol.*, 1950, **45**, 583–591.

Boyd, G. F., "The Levels of Aspiration of White and Negro Children in a Non-Segregated Elementary School," *J. Soc. Psychol.*, 1952, **36**, 191–196.

Bruner, E. M., and J. B. Rotter, "A Level-of-Aspiration Study Among the Ramah Navaho," *J. Pers.*, 1953, **21**, 375–385.

Bryan, W. L., and N. Harter, "Studies in the Physiology and Psychology of the Telegraphic Language," *Psychol. Rev.*, 1897, **4**, 27–53.

Bryan, W. L., and N. Harter, "Studies on the Telegraphic Language. The Acquisition of a Hierarchy of Habits," *Psychol. Rev.*, 1899, **6**, 345–375.

Child, I. L., and J. W. Whitney, "Determinants of Level of Aspiration and Evidence from Everyday Life," *J. Abnorm. Soc. Psychol.*, 1949, **44**, 303–314.

Dembo, T., "Der Anger als Dynamisches Problem," *Psychol. Forsch.*, 1931, **15**, 1–144.

Escalona, Sibylle K., "An Application of the Level of Aspiration Experiment to the Study of Personality," *Teach. Coll. Contr. Educ.*, 1948, No. 937, 132 pp.

Festinger, L., "Wish Expectation, and Group Standards as Factors Influencing Level of Aspiration," *J. Abnorm. Soc. Psychol.*, 1942, **37**, 184–200.

Frank, J. D., "Individual Differences in Certain Aspects of the Level of Aspiration," *Amer. J. Psychol.*, 1935, **47**, 119–128. (a)

Frank, J. D., "Some Psychological Determinants of Level of Aspiration," *Amer. J. Psychol.*, 1935, **47**, 285–293. (b)

Frank, J. D., "The Influence of the Level of Performance in One Task on the Level of Aspiration in Another," *J. Exp. Psychol.*, 1935, **18**, 159–171. (c)

French, J. R. P., Jr., "Field Experiments: Changing Group Productivity," in J. G. Miller (Ed.), *Experiments in Social Process*. New York: McGraw-Hill, Inc., 1950, Ch. 6.

Gardner, J. W., "The Use of the Term 'Level of Aspiration'," *Psychol. Rev.* 1940, **47**, 59–68.

Gould, R., "An Experimental Analysis of Level of Aspiration," *Genet. Psychol. Monogr.*, 1939, **21**, 1–115.

Gulliksen, H., *Theory of Mental Tests*. New York: John Wiley & Sons, Inc., 1950.

Hanawalt, N. G., C. E. Hamilton, and M. L. Morris, "Level of Aspiration in College Leaders and Nonleaders," *J. Abnorm. Soc. Psychol.*, 1943, **38**, 545–548.

Harvey, O. J., and M. Sherif, "Level of Aspiration as a Case of Judgmental Activity in Which Ego-Involvement Operates as Factors," *Sociometry*, 1951, **14**, 141–147.

Hausmann, M. F., "A Test to Evaluate Some Personality Traits," *J. Gen. Psychol.*, 1933, **9**, 179–189.

Hecht, Irving, "The Difference in Goal Striving Behavior Between Peptic Ulcer and Ulcerative Colitis Patients as Evaluated by Psychological Techniques," *J. Clin. Psychol.*, 1952, **8**, 262–265.

Heller, F. A., "Measuring Motivation in Industry," *Occup. Psychol.*, 1952, **26**, 86–95.

Hertzman, M., and L. Festinger, "Shifts in Explicit Goals in a Level of Aspiration Experiment," *J. Exp. Psychol.*, 1940, **27**, 439–452.

Hilgard, E. R., E. M. Sait, and G. A. Margaret, "Level of Aspiration as Affected by Relative Standing in an Experimental Social Group," *J. Exp. Psychol.*, 1940, **27**, 411–421.

Himmelweit, H. T., "A Comparative Study of the Level of Aspiration of Normal and Neurotic Persons," *Brit. J. Psychol.*, 1947, **37**, 11–59

Holt, R. B., "Level of Aspiration: Ambition or Defense?" *J. Exp. Psychol.*, 1946, **36**, 398–416.

Hoppe, F., "Erfolg and Misserfolg," *Psychol. Forsch.*, 1930, **44**, 1–62.

Horwitz, M., R. V. Exline, M. Goldman, and F. J. Lee, *Motivational Effects of Alternative Decision-Making Processes in Groups*, Bureau of Educational Research, Univ. Illinois, 1953.

Irwin, F. W., "The Realism of Expectations," *Psychol. Rev.*, 1944, **51**, 120–126.

Irwin, F. W., and M. C. Mintzer, "Effect of Differences in Instructions and Motivation Upon Measures of the Level of Aspiration," *Amer. J. Psychol.*, 1942, **55**, 400–406.

Jost, K. C., "The Level of Aspiration of Schizophrenics and Normal Subjects," *J. Abnorm. Soc. Psychol.*, 1955, **50**, 315–320.

Jucknat, M., "Performance and Level of Aspiration," *Psychol. Forsch.*, 1937, **22**, 89–177.

Kausler, D. H., "Aspiration Level as a Determinant of Performance," *J. Pers.*, 1959, **27**, 346–351.

Kausler, D. H., and E. P. Trapp, "Achievement Motivation and Goal Setting Behavior on a Learning Task," *J. Exp. Psychol.*, 1958, **55**, 575–578.

Keller, F. S., "Studies in International Morse Code: I. A New Method of Teaching Code Reception," *J. Appl. Psychol.*, 1943, **27**, 407–415.

Keller, F. S., "The Phantom Plateau," *J. Exp. Anal. Behav.*, 1958, **1**, 1–13.

Keller, F. S., "Personal Communication," 1959.

Keller, F. S., and R. E. Taubman, "Studies in International Morse Code: II. Errors Made in Code Reception," *J. Appl. Psychol.*, 1943, **27**, 504–509.

Klein, G. S., "Self-Appraisal of Test Performance as a Vocational Selection Device," *Educ. Psychol. Measmt.*, 1948, **8,** 69–84.

Klugman, S. F., "Emotional Stability and Level of Aspiration," *J. Gen. Psychol.*, 1948, **38,** 101–118.

Kogan, L. S., "Applications of Variance-Covariance Designs in Educational Research," *Rev. of Educ. Research*, 1954, **24,** 439–447.

Kurtz, A. K., "Recent Developments, Practices, and Research in the Field of Code Learning," New York: The Psychological Corporation, 1959. Tech. Rep. No. 1, Contract Nonr-2519 (00).

Lerea, L., "An Exploratory Study on the Effects of Experimentally Induced Success and Failure Upon the Oral Reading Performance and the Levels of Aspiration of Stutterers," *Dissertation Abstr.*, 1954, **14,** 2401.

Lewin, K., T. Dembo, L. Festinger, and P. S. Sears, "Level of Aspiration." In J. Mc. V. Hunt (Ed.) *Personality and the Behavior Disorders*, New York: The Ronald Press Company, 1944, Vol. I., pp. 333–378.

Lindquist, E. L., *Design and Analysis of Experiments*, Boston: Houghton Mifflin, 1953.

Lockette, R. E., "The Effect of Level of Aspiration Upon the Learning of Skills," Unpublished doctor's dissertation, Univ. of Illinois, 1956.

MacIntosh, A., "Differential Effect of the Status of the Competing Group Upon the Levels of Aspiration," *Amer. J. Psychol.*, 1942, **55,** 546–554.

Margaret, A., "Influence of Active Participation in a Social Group Upon Expressed Level of Aspiration," *Psychol. Bull.*, 1942, **39,** 477.

Mast, Vernie, R., "Level of Aspiration as a Method of Studying the Personality of Adult Stutterers," *Speech Monogr.*, 1952, **19,** 196.

McGehee, W., "Judgment and Level of Aspiration," *J. Gen. Psychol.*, 1940, **22,** 3–15.

McGehee, W., "Are we Using What we Know About Training? Learning Theory and Training," *Personnel Psychol.*, 1958, **11,** 1–12.

McNemar, Q., *Psychological Statistics*, New York: John Wiley & Sons, Inc., 1955.

Mischel, W., "The Effect of the Commitment Situation on the Generalization of Expectancies," *J. Pers.*, 1958, **26,** 508–516.

Pennington, L. A., "Shifts in Aspirational Level after Success and Failure in the College Classroom," *J. Gen. Psychol.*, 1940, **23**, 305–313.

Pierce, K. K., "The Personality Inventory Correlates of the Level of Aspiration," *Dissertation Abstr.*, 1954, **14**, 1102–1103.

Preston, M. G., and J. A. Bayton, "Correlations Between Levels of Aspiration," *J. Psychol.*, 1942, **13**, 369–373.

Preston, M. G., A. Spiers, and J. Trasoff, "On Certain Conditions Controlling the Realism and Irrealism of Aspirations," *J. Exp. Psychol.*, 1947, **37**, 48–58.

Ricciuti, H. N., *A Review of Procedural Variations in Level of Aspiration Studies*, Human Resources Research Center Bulletin 51–24, Lackland AFB, San Antonio, 1951.

Ricciuti, H. N., and D. G. Schultz, *Development of Group Measures of Level of Aspiration, An Exploratory Study*, Human Resources Research Center Bulletin 53–51, Lackland AFB, San Antonio, 1953.

Rosenthal, D., and C. N. Cofer, "The Effect on Group Performance of an Indifferent and Neglectful Attitude Shown by One Group Member," *J. Exp. Psychol.*, 1948, **38**, 568–577.

Rotter, J. B., "Level of Aspiration as a Method of Studying Personality: I. A Critical Review of Methodology," *Psychol. Rev.* 1942, **49**, 463–474. (a)

Rotter, J. B., "Level of Aspiration as a Method of Studying Personality: II. Development and Evaluation of a Controlled Method," *J. Exp. Psychol.*, 1942, **31**, 410–422. (b)

Rotter, J. B., "Level of Aspiration as a Method of Studying Personality: III. Group Validity Studies," *Character & Pers.*, 1943, **11**, 254–274.

Rotter, J. B., "Level of Aspiration as a Method of Studying Personality: IV. The Analysis of Patterns of Response," *J. Soc. Psychol.*, 1945, **21**, 159–177.

Rutledge, L., "Aspirational Levels of Deaf Children as Compared With Those of Hearing Children," *J. Speech Hearing Disorders*, 1954, **19**, 375–380.

Sears, P. S., "Level of Aspiration in Academically Successful and Unsuccessful Children," *J. Abnorm. Soc. Psychol.*, 1940, **35**, 498–536.

Sheehan, J. G., and S. L. Zelen, "Level of Aspiration in Stutterers and Nonstutterers," *J. Abnorm. Soc. Psychol.*, 1955, **51,** 83–86.

Simon, J. R., M. E. Shaw, and J. C. Gilchrist, "Some Effects of Pre-arranged Performance Scores Upon the Level of Aspiration," *J. Exp. Psychol.*, 1954, **47,** 10–12.

Sinha, S., "The Experimental Study of the Level of Aspiration," *J. Educ. & Psychol.*, *Baroda*, 1955, **13,** 91–96.

Spragg, S. D. S., "The Relative Difficulty of Morse Code Alphabet Characters Learned by the Whole Method," *J. Exp. Psychol.*, 1943, **33,** 108–114.

Staff, Personnel Research Section, Classification and Replacement Branch, AGO. "The Selection of Radiotelegraph Operators," *Psychol. Bull.*, 1943, **40,** 357–371.

Steisel, I. M., and B. D. Cohen, "The Effects of Two Degrees of Failure on Level of Aspiration and Performance," *J. Abnorm. Soc. Psychol.*, 1951, **46,** 79–82.

Stevens, P. W., "The Performance of Delinquent and Non-Delinquent Defectives in a Level of Aspiration Experiment," *U.N.C. Rec.*, 1952, No. 506,224.

Sutcliffe, J. P., "Responsiveness of the Level of Aspiration to Success and Failure as a Function of Task Variability," *Aust. J. Psychol.*, 1955, **7,** 34–44.

Taylor, D. W., "Learning Telegraphic Code," *Psychol. Bull.*, 1943, **40,** 461–487.

West, L. J., *Review of Research on Morse Code Learning.* Training Aids Research Laboratory, Air Force Personnel and Training Research Center, Air Research and Development Command, Chanute Air Force Base, Illinois, 1955. Research AFPTRC-TN-55-52.

Windle, C., M. Sidman, and F. S. Keller, *Studies in Radiotelegraphy.* Unpublished manuscript, Columbia Univ., 1953.

Wolfle, D., "Military Training and the Useful Parts of Learning Theory," *J. Consult. Psychol.*, 1946, **10,** 73–75.

Wolfle, D., "Training," in S. S. Stevens (Ed.), *Handbook of Experimental Psychology.* New York: John Wiley & Sons, Inc., 1951, pp. 1267–1286.

Yacorzynski, G. K., "Degree of Effort. III. Relationship to the Level of Aspiration," *J. Exp. Psychol.*, 1941, **30,** 407–413.

APPENDIX A

Activity Check List Used to Identify (and Excuse from the Study) Those Students Who Had Prior Experience with International Morse Code

$\longleftarrow$ ——————————— $8\frac{1}{2}''$ ——————————— $\longrightarrow$

Name———————————————— Class————————————————

Please check those activities in which you have participated:

_____Armed Forces   _____Ham Radio Operator

_____Aviation Club   _____Morse Code Reception

_____Boy Scouts   _____R.O.T.C. Summer Camp

_____Civil Air Patrol   _____Science Club

_____Electronics Club   _____Signal Flag Activities

If in Armed Forces, specify branch and your specialty rating:

_____

11"

Complete Script of Training Tapes Used in the Study

The vertical lines at the left of the page indicate the specific experimental group(s) which heard the script of the tape listed on the immediate right. The ten experimental groups are coded as follows:

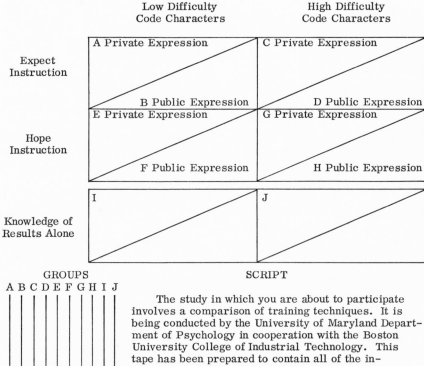

	Low Difficulty Code Characters	High Difficulty Code Characters
Expect Instruction	A Private Expression / B Public Expression	C Private Expression / D Public Expression
Hope Instruction	E Private Expression / F Public Expression	G Private Expression / H Public Expression
Knowledge of Results Alone	I	J

GROUPS

A B C D E F G H I J

SCRIPT

The study in which you are about to participate involves a comparison of training techniques. It is being conducted by the University of Maryland Department of Psychology in cooperation with the Boston University College of Industrial Technology. This tape has been prepared to contain all of the instructions which you are to follow. Since your results will be compared to the results of other groups, it is imperative that you follow the instructions as given.

You will have to pay close attention throughout the study. Furthermore, your success will in large part be dependent upon your alertness in following the instructions. Throughout the study you are to talk with no one. The papers which have been handed to you will be explained to you later.

A B C D E F G H I J

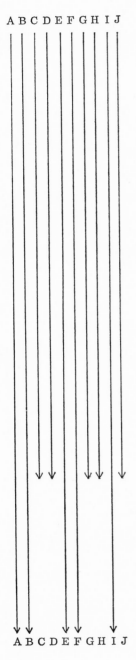

A B C D E F G H I J

A B C D E F G H I J

More specifically, this study involves the learning of International Morse Code. The International Morse Code is a special language used for transmitting messages. It consists of combinations of sound which stand for, or are equivalent to, the letters of the alphabet. The combinations involve both short and long sounds; namely, the "dit" (a "dit" is sounded) called a short sound, and the "dah" (a "dah" is sounded), the long sound.

To reduce errors when working with International Morse Code, it is important to always use the phonetic alphabet. This alphabet merely consists of each name beginning with the letter it represents, and has been chosen since it has a unique and distinctive sound. For example, the letter A is not called "A", rather it is called ALFA. The letter B is called BRAVO, and C is called COCOA, and so on through the entire alphabet. By this means, there is less likelihood of confusing letters with each other.

Today's study involves nine specific letters of the alphabet. In code work the letters are sometimes called code characters. The letters have been listed on the blackboard. DO NOT write them down, since they have been placed on the blackboard for your convenience and ready reference.

In this study you are to respond _every_ time you hear a code character. Your response is to be placed on the sheets in the booklet on your chair. You'll notice that each sheet consists of several groups of blocks, each block containing ten squares. Each time after you hear the signal, you are to print the letter it represents in one of the squares. At this point, use only the top row of each block and work across the page from left to right. Thus the first sheet of your booklet gives you space to respond to 45 signals, since there are nine blocks, each block allowing you to respond five times.

You will first hear the phonetic name of each letter followed by the vocal sound of the code character. Lastly, you will hear the code character as a radio operator hears it. This signal will be repeated five times. Remember to print the letter each time you hear the signal. I'll repeat that, print the letter each time you hear the signal. The first letter is E for ECHO. Here is the vocal sound for the code character for ECHO, "dit," and now the signal given five times: (signal is sounded five times with a 4-second inter-signal interval). You should have printed the letter E, meaning ECHO, each

A B C D E F G H I J

time you heard the signal, and so the first block
of squares should consist of five E's in the top
row. (5-second pause) Now follow the same procedure for each of the other letters. The next
letter is:

  T for TANGO. The vocal sound is "dah" and
    now the signal. (signal is sounded five
    times with 4-second inter-signal inter-
    val)
  M for METRO.   "dah-dah" (signal is sounded
    five times with same interval)
  I for INDIA   "dit-dit"   (signal
  A for ALFA   "dit-dah"   always
  N for NECTAR   "dah-dit"   sounded
  R for ROMEO   "dit-dah-dit"   five times
  B for BRAVO   "dah-dit-dit-dit" with same
  H for HOTEL   "dit-dit-dit-dit" interval)

Now turn the sheet and use the second page.
Once again the signals, and be sure to print the
letter each time you hear the signal.

  E for ECHO
  T for TANGO
  M for METRO
  I for INDIA   (as before, the vocal sound is
  A for ALFA   given and the signal is sounded
  N for NECTAR   five times)
  R for ROMEO
  B for BRAVO
  H for HOTEL

Now turn the page and you can continue to practice on the third page. This time, however, the
letters will be repeated without the vocal sounds.
As soon as you hear the code character, print the
letter in the next space on your practice sheet.
Ready (a "dit" is sounded, followed by a 4-second
pause). You should have printed the letter E for
ECHO. If you printed some other letter, or if you
didn't print any letter at all in the space, print
the letter E in the space directly below. (5-sec-
ond pause) Thus the top row of each block of
squares will represent your initial response to the
signal. The bottom row will represent the correct
response to the signal, to be filled in only if
your original response was in error. An example
of a response sheet has been placed on the blackboard to clarify the system of responding. Looking at the example, it will be noticed that the
first signal sounded was ALFA; and the student

A B C D E F G H I J

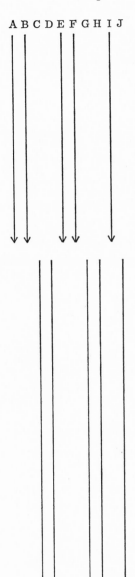

A B C D E F G H I J

A B C D E F G H I J

responded correctly by placing the letter A in the top square. The student missed the next signal and so drew a dash in the second square. Notice however, that upon hearing the announcer identify the signal as N for NECTAR, the student then printed the letter N in the square directly below. The third signal was T for TANGO and was correctly identified. The fourth signal was identified by the student as A for ALFA; however, the announcer identified the signal as N for NECTAR, and so the student noted his error by printing the letter N in the square directly below. The fifth signal was T for TANGO, and the student responded correctly. Thus this procedure allows you to quickly score your paper, and this same procedure will be followed throughout the remainder of the study. It is imperative that you understand it exactly. Are there any questions at all? (15-second pause)

You will first hear the phonetic name of each letter followed by the vocal sound of the code character. Lastly, you will hear the code character as a radio operator hears it. This signal will be repeated five times. Remember to print the letter each time you hear the signal. I'll repeat that, print the letter each time you hear the signal. The first letter is W for WHISKEY, "dit-dah-dah," and now the signal given five times: (signal is sounded five times with a 4-second inter-signal interval) You should have printed the letter W, meaning WHISKEY, each time you heard the signal, and so the first block of squares should consist of five W's in the top row. (5-second pause) Now follow the same procedure for each of the other letters. The next letter is:

J for JULIETT. The vocal sound is "dit-dah-dah-dah" and now the signal. (signal is sounded five times with 4-second inter-signal interval)

P for PAPA. "dit-dah-dah-dit" (signal is sounded five times with same interval)

L for LIMA   "dit-dah-dit-dit"   (signal
U for UNION   "dit-dit-dah"   always
F for FOXTROT "dit-dit-dah-dit"   sounded
Y for YANKEE   "dah-dit-dah-dah" five times
X for XTRA   "dah-dit-dit-dah" with same
Q for QUEBEC   "dah-dah-dit-dah" interval)

Now turn the sheet and use the second page. Once again the signals, and be sure to print the letter each time you hear the signal.

ABCDEFGHIJ

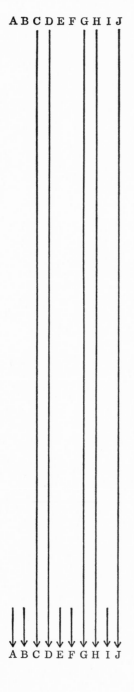

W for WHISKEY
J for JULIETT
P for PAPA   (as before, the vocal
L for LIMA   sound is given and the
U for UNION   signal is sounded
F for FOXTROT   five times)
Y for YANKEE
X for XTRA
Q for QUEBEC

Now turn the page and you can continue to
practice on the third page. This time, however,
the letters will be repeated without the vocal
sounds. As soon as you hear the code character,
print the letter in the next space on your practice sheet. Ready (a "dit-dah-dah" is sounded,
followed by a 4-second pause). You should have
printed the letter W for WHISKEY. If you printed
some other letter, or if you didn't print any letter at all in the space, print the letter W in
the space directly below. (5-second pause) Thus
the top row of each block of squares will represent
your initial response to the signal. The bottom
row will represent the correct response to the
signal, to be filled in only if your original response was in error. An example of a response
sheet has been placed on the blackboard to clarify
the system of responding. Looking at the example,
it will be noticed that the first signal sounded
was LIMA; and the student responded correctly by
placing the letter L in the top square. The student
missed the next signal and so drew a dash in the
second square. Notice, however, that upon hearing
the announcer identify the signal as Q for QUEBEC,
the student then printed the letter Q in the square
directly below. The third signal was P for PAPA
and was correctly identified. The fourth signal
was identified by the student as L for LIMA; however, the announcer identified the signal as Q
for QUEBEC, and so the student noted his error by
printing the letter Q in the square directly below.
The fifth signal was P for PAPA, and the student
responded correctly. Thus this procedure allows
you to quickly score you paper, and this procedure
will be followed throughout the remainder of the
study. It is imperative that you understand it
exactly. Are there any questions at all? (15-
second pause)

Remember that your task will be to master the
learning of these nine code characters. A test
will be given at the end of the period to measure

ABCDEFGHIJ

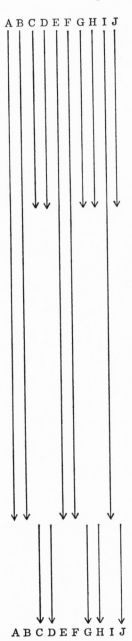

A B C D E F G H I J

A B C D E F G H I J

your learning; furthermore, the test section will not include the correct answer being given by the announcer. Thus, in your training session, you will want to anticipate the identification of the signal by the announcer. For this reason, a short time delay is given before identification of the signal so that you can respond before the signal is identified. This requirement to anticipate the identification of the signal will assist you in your learning of the signals. Further, do not wait until the announcer has identified the signal before responding on the top row. The proctor will be monitoring you to check this behavior, since failure to anticipate the signal will not prepare you for the final test.

Now let's continue the training session on the same page. You will now hear another code character. Print the letter in the next square on your practice sheet. Ready (a "dah" is sounded, followed by a 4-second pause). You should have printed T for TANGO. If you printed some other letter, print the letter T in the square directly below. Now the next letter:

("dah-dah" is sounded) that was	M for METRO
("dit-dit" is sounded)	I for INDIA
("dit-dah" is sounded)	A for ALFA
("dah-dit" is sounded)	N for NECTAR
("dah-dah-dit" is sounded)	R for ROMEO
("dah-dit-dit-dit" is sounded)	B for BRAVO
("dit-dit-dit-dit" is sounded)	H for HOTEL
("dit-dit-dit-dit" is sounded)	H for HOTEL
("dah-dit-dit-dit" is sounded)	B for BRAVO
("dit-dah-dit" is sounded)	R for ROMEO
("dah-dit" is sounded)	N for NECTAR
("dit-dah" is sounded)	A for ALFA
("dit-dit" is sounded)	I for INDIA
("dah-dah" is sounded)	M for METRO
("dah" is sounded)	T for TANGO
("dit" is sounded)	E for ECHO

Now let's continue the training session on the same page. You will now hear another code character. Print the letter in the next square on your practice sheet. Ready (a "dit-dah-dah-dah" is sounded, followed by a 4-second pause). You should have printed J for JULIETT. If you printed some other letter, print the letter J in the square directly below. Now the next letter:

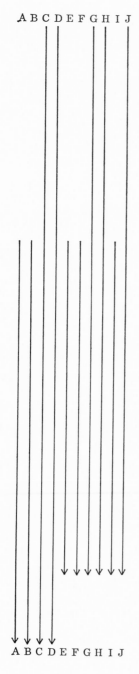

A B C D E F G H I J

("dit-dah-dah-dit" is sounded) that was P for	PAPA
("dit-dah-dit-dit" is sounded)	L for LIMA
("dit-dit-dah" is sounded)	U for UNION
("dit-dit-dah-dit" is sounded)	F for FOXTROT
("dah-dit-dah-dah" is sounded)	Y for YANKEE
("dah-dit-dit-dah" is sounded)	X for XTRA
("dah-dah-dit-dah" is sounded)	Q for QUEBEC
("dah-dah-dit-dah" is sounded)	Q for QUEBEC
("dah-dit-dit-dah" is sounded)	X for XTRA
("dah-dit-dah-dah" is sounded)	Y for YANKEE
("dit-dit-dah-dit" is sounded)	F for FOXTROT
("dit-dit-dah" is sounded)	U for UNION
("dit-dah-dit-dit" is sounded)	L for LIMA
("dit-dah-dah-dit" is sounded)	P for PAPA
("dit-dah-dah-dah" is sounded)	J for JULIETT
("dit-dah-dah" is sounded)	W for WHISKEY

Now turn the page and the regular training trials will begin. The signals will appear in a random order; that is, they will not follow a uniform pattern of appearing. There will be 15 training trials, each containing 25 signals. A short rest period will be allowed after training trial No. 7. Ready.

(Training Trial No. 1 is presented)

You will now score your own sheet for that trial of 25 signals. Count the number of entries on the <u>bottom</u> row of each block of squares. Subtract this number from 25 and enter the score in the space at the bottom of the sheet marked "score." Since 25 is a perfect score, your entry should reflect how many of the 25 signals were <u>correctly</u> identified on the top row of each block of squares. (15-second pause) Turn the page and the training session will continue. Ready for training trial No. 2.

(Training Trial No. 2 is presented)

Again, score your sheet by subtracting the number of errors – that is, entries on the bottom row – from 25. Enter the score in the space provided. (10-second pause) Now turn the page.

In addition, we want you to set the score you <u>expect</u> to make on this next training trial of 25 signals. Do <u>not</u> set the score you hope to make, nor the score you think you will not go below, but rather indicate the exact score you expect to make–

A B C D E F G H I J

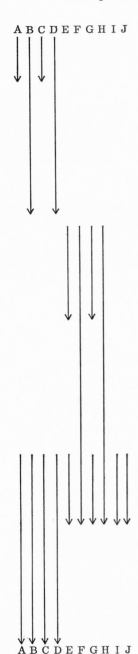

A B C D E F G H I J

that is, your expectation for this trial. Write
that expectation on the top line which says,
"The score I expect to make on this trial is ____."
(4-second pause)

The proctor will be recording the expectation
of each member of the entire group. These will be
listed on the blackboard next to your individual
seat numbers. You will be responding by sequential
seat numbers, with the beginning point in the
sequence systematically rotated. The person in
seat number 1 will now call out the expectation he
entered on his sheet, followed by seat number 2,
number 3, and so forth in sequence. (30-second
pause)

In addition, we want you to set the score you
hope to make on this next training trial of 25
signals. Do not set the score you expect to make,
nor the score you think you will not go below, but
rather indicate the exact score you hope to make –
that is, your goal for this trial. Write that
goal on the top line which says, "The score I hope
to make on this trial is ____." (4-second pause)

The proctor will be recording the hope of
each member of the entire group. These will be
listed on the blackboard next to your individual
seat numbers. You will be responding by sequential seat numbers, with the beginning point in the
sequence systematically rotated. The person in
seat number 1 will now call out the hope he entered
on his sheet, followed by seat number 2, number 3,
and so forth in sequence. (30-second pause)

Ready for training trial No. 3.

(Training Trial No. 3 is presented)

Determine your score, enter it in the space
provided. (10-second pause) Now turn the page.

Knowing your score on that last trial, set
the exact score you expect to make on this next
trial. Remember, not the score you hope to make,
not the score you feel sure you will not go below, but the exact score you expect to make –– in
other words, your expectation for this trial.
Write that expectation on the top line which says,
"The score I expect to make on this trial is
____." (4-second pause)

A B C D E F G H I J

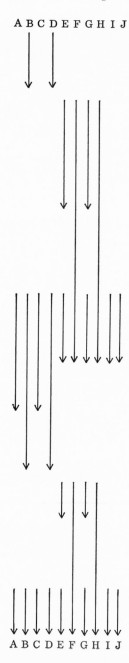

A B C D E F G H I J

The proctor will again record the expectation entered on the sheet by each member of the group. This time, the person in seat number 2 will lead off, followed by seat number 3, number 4, and so forth in sequence. (30-second pause)

Knowing your score on that last trial, set the exact score you hope to make on this next trial. Remember, not the score you expect to make, not the score you feel sure you will not go below, but the exact score you hope to make -- in other words, your goal for this trial. Write that goal on the top line which says, "The score I hope to make on this trial is ___." (4-second pause)

The proctor will again record the hope entered on the sheet by each member of the group. This time the person in seat number 2 will lead off, followed by seat number 3, number 4, and so forth in sequence. (30-second pause)

Ready for training trial No. 4.

(Training Trial No. 4 is presented)

Determine your score, enter it in the space provided. (10-second pause) Now turn the page.

Think over what score you expect to make on this trial. Enter it in the space on the top of the sheet. (2-second pause)

Again the proctor will record the expectation of each member of the group. This time, the person in seat number 3 will lead off, followed in sequence by number 4, 5, and so forth. (30-second pause)

Think over what score you hope to make on this trial. Enter it in the space on the top of the sheet. (2-second pause)

Again the proctor will record the hope of each member of the group. This time, the person in seat number 3 will lead off, followed in sequence by number 4, 5, and so forth. (30-second pause)

Ready for training trial No. 5.

(Training Trial No. 5 is presented)

A B C D E F G H I J

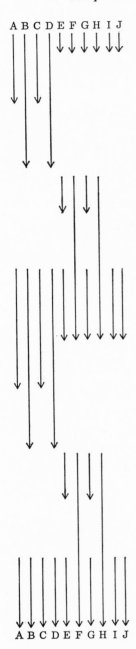

Determine your score, enter it in the space provided. (10-second pause) Now turn the page.

Think over what score you expect to make on this trial. Enter it in the space provided. (2-second pause)

Again the proctor will record the expectation of each member of the group. This time, the person in seat number 4 will lead off. (30-second pause)

Think over what score you hope to make on this trial. Enter it in the space provided. (2-second pause)

Again the proctor will record the hope of each member of the group. This time, the person in seat number 4 will lead off. (30-second pause)

Ready for training trial No. 6.

(Training Trial No. 6 is presented)

Determine your score, enter it in the space provided. (10-second pause) Now turn the page.

Think over what score you expect to make on this trial. Enter it in the space provided. (2-second pause)

Again the proctor will record the expectation of each member of the group. This time, the person in seat number 5 will lead off. (30-second pause)

Think over what score you hope to make on this trial. Enter it in the space provided. (2-second pause)

Again the proctor will record the hope of each member of the group. This time, the person in seat number 5 will lead off. (30-second pause)

Ready for training trial No. 7.

(Training Trial No. 7 is presented)

Determine your score, enter it in the space provided. (10-second pause) Now turn the page.

A B C D E F G H I J

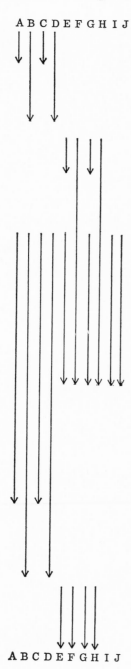

Think over what score you <u>expect</u> to make on this trial. Enter it in the space provided. (2-second pause)

Again the proctor will record the expectation of each member of the group. This time, the person in seat number 6 will lead off. (30-second pause)

Think over what score you <u>hope</u> to make on this trial. Enter it in the space provided. (2-second pause)

Again the proctor will record the hope of each member of the group. This time, the person in seat number 6 will lead off. (30-second pause)

Before going on to the next session, you will now take a 5-minute rest period. During this time you are to remain silent and you are not to leave your seat. (5-minute pause)

Ready for training trial No. 8.

(Training Trial No. 8 is presented)

Determine your score by subtracting the number of errors from 25. Enter the score in the space provided. (10-second pause) Now turn the page.

Knowing your score on that last trial, set the exact score you <u>expect</u> to make on this next trial. Remember, not the score you hope to make, not the score you feel sure you will not go below, but the exact score you <u>expect</u> to make -- in other words, your expectation for this trial. Write that expectation on the top line which says, "The score I <u>expect</u> to make on this trial is ____." (2-second pause)

The proctor will again record the expectation entered on the sheet by each member of the group. This time, the person in seat number 7 will lead off, followed by seat number 8, number 9, and so forth in sequence. (30-second pause)

Knowing your score on that last trial, set the exact score you <u>hope</u> to make on this next trial. Remember, not the score you expect to make, not the score you feel sure you will not go below, but the exact score you <u>hope</u> to make -- in other words,

A B C D E F G H I J

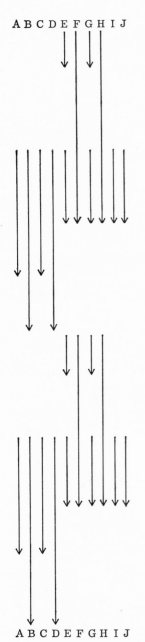

A B C D E F G H I J

A B C D E F G H I J

your goal for this trial. Write that goal on the top line which says, "The score I <u>hope</u> to make on this trial is ____." (2-second pause)

The proctor will again record the hope entered on the sheet by each member of the group. This time the person in seat number 7 will lead off, followed by seat number 8, number 9, and so forth in sequence. (30-second pause)

Ready for training trial No. 9.

(Training Trial No. 9 is presented)

Determine your score, enter it in the space provided. (10-second pause) Now turn the page.

Think over what score you <u>expect</u> to make on this trial. Enter it in the space provided. (2-second pause)

Again the proctor will record the expectation of each member of the group. This time, the person in seat number 8 will lead off. (30-second pause)

Think over what score you <u>hope</u> to make on this trial. Enter it in the space provided. (2-second pause)

Again the proctor will record the hope of each member of the group. This time the person in seat number 8 will lead off. (30-second pause)

Ready for training trial No. 10.

(Training Trial No. 10 is presented)

Determine your score, enter it in the space provided. (10-second pause) Now turn the page.

Think over what score you <u>expect</u> to make on this trial. Enter it in the space provided. (2-second pause)

Again the proctor will record the expectation of each member of the group. This time the person in seat number 9 will lead off. (30-second pause)

A B C D E F G H I J

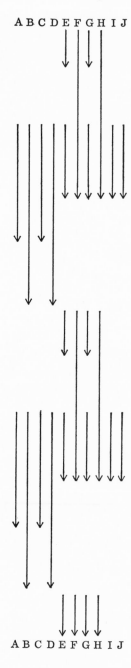

Think over what score you <u>hope</u> to make on this trial. Enter it in the space provided. (2-second pause)

Again the proctor will record the hope of each member of the group. This time the person in seat number 9 will lead off. (30-second pause)

Ready for training trial No. 11.

(Training Trial No. 11 is presented)

Determine your score, enter it in the space provided. (10-second pause) Now turn the page.

Think over what score you <u>expect</u> to make on this trial. Enter it in the space provided. (2-second pause)

Again the proctor will record the expectation of each member of the group. This time the person in seat number 10 will lead off. (30-second pause)

Think over what score you <u>hope</u> to make on this trial. Enter it in the space provided. (2-second pause)

Again the proctor will record the hope of each member of the group. This time the person in seat number 10 will lead off. (30-second pause)

Ready for training trial No. 12.

(Training Trial No. 12 is presented)

Determine your score, enter it in the space provided. (10-second pause) Now turn the page.

Think over what score you <u>expect</u> to make on this trial. Enter it in the space provided. (2-second pause)

Again the proctor will record the expectation of each member of the group. This time the person in seat number 3 will lead off. (30-second pause)

Think over what score you <u>hope</u> to make on this trial. Enter it in the space provided. (2-second pause)

A B C D E F G H I J

A B C D E F G H I J

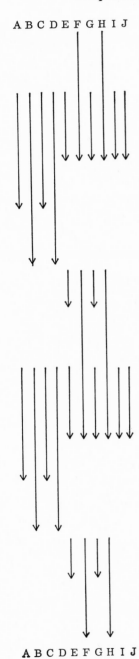

Again the proctor will record the hope of each member of the group. This time the person in seat number 3 will lead off. (30-second pause)

Ready for training trial No. 13.

(Training Trial No. 13 is presented)

Determine your score, enter it in the space provided. (10-second pause) Now turn the page.

Think over what score you <u>expect</u> to make on this trial. Enter it in the space provided. (2-second pause)

Again the proctor will record the expectation of each member of the group. This time the person in seat number 5 will lead off. (30-second pause)

Think over what score you <u>hope</u> to make on this trial. Enter it in the space provided. (2-second pause)

Again the proctor will record the hope of each member of the group. This time the person in seat number 5 will lead off. (30-second pause)

Ready for training trial No. 14.

(Training Trial No. 14 is presented)

Determine your score, enter it in the space provided. (10-second pause) Now turn the page.

Think over what score you <u>expect</u> to make on this trial. Enter it in the space provided. (2-second pause)

Again the proctor will record the expectation of each member of the group. This time the person in seat number 7 will lead off. (30-second pause)

Think over what score you <u>hope</u> to make on this trial. Enter it in the space provided. (2-second pause)

Again the proctor will record the hope of each member of the group. This time the person in seat number 7 will lead off. (30-second pause)

A B C D E F G H I J

A B C D E F G H I J

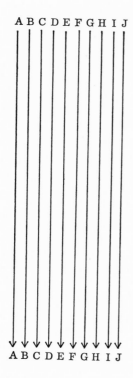

A B C D E F G H I J

Ready for your last training trial, No. 15.

(Training Trial No. 15 is presented)

Determine your score, enter it in the space provided. (10-second pause) Now turn the page and stand by.

Your training session is now complete, and a short test will be administered. As indicated previously, the announcer will not identify each signal for you. Rather, you will be responding to the signal without the benefit of this identification. Ready for the test.

(Test of 45 signals is presented)

We want to thank you for your participation in this doctoral dissertation. Please do not discuss this study with anyone, since your comparison to other groups will be affected. We will be reporting the results of this study to you when the study is completed and the data have been analyzed. However, if you have any questions which might be answered at this time, we are sure the proctor will do his best to answer them. Again our thanks for your participation and cooperation.

Basic Raw Data of the Study

The ten experimental groups are presented in successive alphabetical order. The number in the *right* half of each cell is the number of signals correctly identified during that particular trial in the training session. The number in the *left* half of each cell is the level of aspiration specified by the trainee before starting that particular trial. It will be noticed that no level of aspiration was set for the first two trials by any of the trainees. Finally, the test score for each trainee is presented in the cell adjacent to the Trial Number 15 cell.

GROUP A. "EXPECT" INSTRUCTIONS, "PRIVATE" EXPRESSION, "LOW" DIFFICULTY CODE CHARACTERS

Trainee	Trial #1	Trial #2	Trial #3		Trial #4		Trial #5		Trial #6		Trial #7		Trial #8	
1	9	8	10	6	8	7	9	5	7	11	13	20	18	22
2	12	18	16	13	15	18	17	16	18	18	16	17	19	16
3	16	14	15	15	16	17	17	16	17	16	17	18	17	15
4	5	9	12	8	10	14	12	7	10	10	8	9	10	9
5	7	10	5	7	5	7	8	10	11	13	14	9	10	8
6	10	9	11	7	11	12	11	12	14	10	14	11	14	6
7	14	16	18	13	14	14	16	16	16	14	15	13	14	13
8	9	9	11	12	13	16	15	15	16	12	15	11	14	13
9	12	16	15	12	14	12	13	10	12	15	14	10	12	17
10	20	21	22	22	23	25	25	24	25	25	25	25	25	23

Trainee	Trial #9		Trial #10		Trial #11		Trial #12		Trial #13		Trial #14		Trial #15		Test Score
1	22	22	23	22	23	21	23	19	22	19	22	21	23	22	36
2	18	21	19	19	20	21	19	20	21	20	20	21	21	21	39
3	17	23	20	20	20	22	21	20	21	18	21	20	20	20	29
4	10	11	10	10	10	14	12	15	12	13	15	12	14	14	28
5	10	10	11	7	10	12	10	11	10	12	10	12	12	11	18
6	11	11	11	15	12	17	14	16	15	18	16	15	20	17	31
7	14	17	16	18	16	17	17	20	18	18	16	18	18	22	40
8	16	12	14	14	15	13	15	12	15	12	15	13	18	14	23
9	17	19	18	19	18	19	18	23	20	18	19	17	19	17	33
10	25	24	25	24	25	24	25	25	25	25	25	25	25	23	43

GROUP B. "EXPECT" INSTRUCTIONS, "PUBLIC" EXPRESSION, "LOW" DIFFICULTY CODE CHARACTERS

Trainee	Trial #1	Trial #2	Trial #3		Trial #4		Trial #5		Trial #6		Trial #7		Trial #8	
1	12	14	17	17	19	19	19	19	19	24	23	21	23	24
2	22	24	24	25	25	24	25	24	25	25	25	25	25	25
3	23	24	24	24	25	25	25	24	25	24	25	25	25	24
4	15	13	11	11	11	12	14	12	15	15	17	11	15	9
5	12	10	12	13	14	18	17	17	19	12	18	16	18	20
6	15	17	19	21	22	21	23	24	25	22	25	24	25	21
7	11	9	11	14	14	11	12	14	13	15	16	15	16	16
8	14	17	20	19	20	17	20	19	20	16	18	21	22	17
9	11	15	13	14	12	16	10	17	20	15	14	18	13	19
10	11	11	11	13	13	15	16	14	18	16	20	17	20	17

Trainee	Trial #9		Trial #10		Trial #11		Trial #12		Trial #13		Trial #14		Trial #15		Test Score
1	23	23	24	19	24	25	24	22	24	23	25	24	25	23	40
2	25	25	25	25	25	25	25	25	25	24	25	25	25	25	44
3	25	25	25	25	25	25	25	24	25	25	25	25	25	25	45
4	12	7	10	10	12	14	16	12	14	11	13	18	17	10	23
5	20	19	21	18	22	18	20	18	22	18	21	21	22	22	41
6	24	25	25	24	25	22	25	25	25	25	25	24	25	24	43
7	18	15	16	17	17	18	18	18	19	17	18	18	19	22	15
8	19	18	22	20	22	23	25	22	23	21	22	19	22	22	30
9	23	20	23	23	24	22	24	18	21	21	22	18	20	24	23
10	25	17	17	16	14	16	16	21	18	19	19	20	20	17	31

GROUP C. "EXPECT" INSTRUCTIONS, "PRIVATE" EXPRESSION, "HIGH" DIFFICULTY CODE CHARACTERS

Trainee	Trial #1	Trial #2	Trial #3	Trial #4	Trial #5	Trial #6	Trial #7	Trial #8
1	5	6	5 8	8 7	8 8	8 9	8 10	9 8
2	9	7	9 6	5 5	5 4	5 5	6 9	7 6
3	5	7	7 10	10 11	15 8	14 12	15 13	15 10
4	7	8	9 13	12 12	13 14	14 13	13 18	15 16
5	6	5	5 8	7 8	8 7	7 5	7 7	8 10
6	6	7	6 8	7 7	6 11	8 5	6 7	7 7
7	9	9	9 10	9 7	8 11	10 4	7 12	9 12
8	8	7	9 6	7 8	8 7	8 10	9 9	10 10
9	8	5	5 4	5 6	6 9	8 8	8 12	10 10
10	0	4	8 5	6 4	5 6	6 1	5 6	6 8

Trainee	Trial #9	Trial #10	Trial #11	Trial #12	Trial #13	Trial #14	Trial #15	Test Score
1	9 5	7 11	9 11	11 6	9 7	8 11	10 15	21
2	7 6	6 8	9 8	8 10	11 8	10 11	11 11	11
3	12 12	11 8	10 11	14 13	16 15	17 18	20 19	17
4	16 14	16 18	16 14	16 13	16 18	17 16	18 14	24
5	9 9	10 9	8 11	10 9	9 12	10 12	10 12	13
6	7 10	7 9	7 10	7 11	7 9	7 8	7 9	10
7	10 8	9 7	9 2	9 14	9 14	9 4	9 10	17
8	11 12	11 11	12 14	12 12	13 14	14 14	15 15	32
9	10 12	12 10	11 12	12 8	10 8	8 10	10 11	20
10	7 6	7 6	6 10	7 14	8 8	8 10	9 10	8

GROUP D. "EXPECT" INSTRUCTIONS, "PUBLIC" EXPRESSION, "HIGH" DIFFICULTY CODE CHARACTERS

Trainee	Trial #1	Trial #2	Trial #3	Trial #4	Trial #5	Trial #6	Trial #7	Trial #8
1	5	6	5 5	6 7	7 8	8 8	9 11	10 9
2	4	4	4 5	5 4	5 10	7 3	6 9	7 8
3	5	6	7 4	5 4	6 8	7 5	6 8	7 6
4	13	5	5 7	6 7	7 12	8 12	10 16	13 16
5	6	9	5 10	7 9	5 9	4 5	6 6	6 6
6	10	10	6 9	7 12	9 11	11 12	12 12	12 15
7	3	4	5 3	4 6	5 8	6 6	6 8	7 3
8	10	9	7 9	8 10	9 11	10 12	11 12	12 9
9	11	13	10 13	10 11	10 12	10 11	10 12	10 11
10	2	7	8 3	3 4	5 12	8 13	10 11	10 10

Trainee	Trial #9	Trial #10	Trial #11	Trial #12	Trial #13	Trial #14	Trial #15	Test Score
1	10 10	10 9	10 8	9 8	9 7	8 9	10 2	10
2	7 8	7 7	7 8	7 5	7 4	7 9	7 8	13
3	7 7	7 6	7 7	7 8	7 8	8 11	9 9	12
4	13 17	14 16	14 18	15 16	15 16	16 17	16 18	28
5	5 10	6 3	4 8	5 8	6 8	8 7	6 7	10
6	12 13	13 10	13 14	13 14	14 15	14 14	15 14	23
7	5 7	6 7	7 7	8 10	9 3	8 10	9 8	14
8	9 13	9 12	12 14	12 15	14 15	14 16	15 14	19
9	10 12	10 12	10 14	12 11	10 11	10 16	12 14	17
10	10 12	12 13	13 13	14 14	14 15	15 17	15 15	23

GROUP E. "HOPE" INSTRUCTIONS, "PRIVATE" EXPRESSION, "LOW" DIFFICULTY CODE CHARACTERS

Trainee	Trial #1	Trial #2	Trial #3		Trial #4		Trial #5		Trial #6		Trial #7		Trial #8	
1	13	13	15	12	15	14	16	19	18	16	18	18	19	16
2	14	12	17	15	17	20	21	13	16	16	17	18	19	12
3	15	15	16	16	20	18	20	16	18	17	18	19	20	16
4	20	20	23	21	23	21	25	24	25	24	25	24	25	24
5	13	10	12	12	14	14	15	18	18	19	19	22	23	23
6	10	13	15	14	15	12	16	17	19	14	18	16	18	16
7	9	14	16	15	16	19	20	13	16	16	18	17	18	18
8	12	14	15	16	17	15	17	17	18	18	18	18	19	17
9	15	16	20	17	20	19	20	20	22	13	20	14	20	13
10	6	9	25	7	15	11	15	10	15	8	15	12	20	14

Trainee	Trial #9		Trial #10		Trial #11		Trial #12		Trial #13		Trial #14		Trial #15		Test Score
1	19	16	19	15	19	16	19	18	19	18	19	18	19	15	28
2	16	17	17	21	18	18	20	20	20	20	21	23	24	23	39
3	20	11	20	17	20	18	20	18	25	16	25	20	25	22	31
4	25	25	25	24	25	23	25	24	25	25	25	25	25	23	45
5	25	25	25	24	25	24	25	24	25	25	25	25	25	25	45
6	20	20	22	23	25	22	25	23	25	25	25	23	25	22	43
7	20	20	20	19	21	22	24	23	25	21	25	22	25	21	41
8	19	20	20	17	20	20	21	16	20	21	22	20	23	19	32
9	20	18	20	17	21	20	22	19	22	21	23	22	25	20	32
10	25	10	25	16	25	15	25	13	25	14	25	16	25	17	30

GROUP F. "HOPE" INSTRUCTIONS, "PUBLIC" EXPRESSION, "LOW" DIFFICULTY
CODE CHARACTERS

Trainee	Trial #1		Trial #2		Trial #3		Trial #4		Trial #5		Trial #6		Trial #7		Trial #8	
1	19		13		15	17	18	19	20	15	20	18	21	19	21	19
2	9		9		12	17	15	14	17	14	17	15	17	18	19	17
3	13		15		25	13	25	16	25	17	25	18	25	17	25	14
4	15		19		23	22	25	23	25	22	25	23	25	22	25	24
5	9		10		15	7	15	13	17	12	25	11	20	9	15	8
6	14		12		15	13	15	13	15	14	15	16	17	17	18	14
7	24		22		25	22	25	22	25	23	25	23	25	23	25	24
8	14		13		15	15	16	13	16	15	16	14	19	17	17	17
9	9		1ł		16	15	16	12	16	13	16	14	17	15	17	13
10	18		17		17	23	20	21	20	21	21	20	21	24	25	22

Trainee	Trial #9		Trial #10		Trial #11		Trial #12		Trial #13		Trial #14		Trial #15		Test Score
1	21	21	23	22	25	20	25	22	25	19	24	18	25	22	35
2	19	19	20	21	22	20	22	21	22	22	25	22	25	20	31
3	25	15	25	14	25	13	25	17	25	18	25	18	25	17	31
4	25	23	20	21	25	23	25	24	25	19	25	19	25	19	32
5	15	8	18	17	23	12	20	12	25	12	23	12	21	10	25
6	18	19	19	16	19	11	19	15	19	16	19	17	19	20	31
7	25	19	25	23	25	23	25	22	25	23	25	22	25	24	42
8	20	15	20	16	16	11	18	14	25	16	25	14	25	19	27
9	17	15	17	17	20	20	22	22	25	17	23	20	24	18	36
10	23	23	25	25	25	24	25	25	25	23	25	25	25	25	33

Trainee	Trial #1	Trial #2	Trial #3		Trial #4		Trial #5		Trial #6		Trial #7		Trial #8	
1	7	7	8	10	10	8	10	13	14	10	12	12	12	13
2	8	9	12	7	10	11	13	12	14	10	13	7	11	8
3	4	5	8	8	10	11	12	12	15	11	14	16	16	15
4	7	1	5	2	4	10	10	8	10	7	10	14	15	12
5	5	9	11	9	11	12	14	16	18	15	18	16	18	13
6	8	6	8	6	8	6	8	14	15	8	10	13	13	10
7	8	7	8	7	8	7	8	8	9	8	9	10	10	9
8	2	3	7	7	8	3	5	5	6	6	7	5	7	13
9	9	5	4	4	5	6	6	4	4	7	7	10	10	8
10	11	10	13	11	12	12	13	11	13	14	15	16	17	16

Trainee	Trial #9		Trial #10		Trial #11		Trial #12		Trial #13		Trial #14		Trial #15		Test Score
1	12	16	14	16	14	16	16	15	15	12	5	13	20	19	14
2	10	13	14	11	14	8	14	15	15	10	15	11	15	9	10
3	18	13	16	16	18	14	18	14	18	13	18	14	18	11	14
4	15	13	15	14	15	15	15	20	20	18	20	19	20	21	30
5	18	17	18	14	18	18	20	19	20	22	25	22	25	20	37
6	13	13	15	13	15	15	17	15	17	16	17	16	17	16	15
7	10	11	12	8	10	10	12	10	10	6	8	9	10	5	12
8	15	4	6	7	10	8	10	8	10	14	15	9	10	9	13
9	9	5	8	4	10	7	10	5	10	7	10	13	13	9	20
10	17	16	17	14	17	16	17	19	20	18	20	21	22	18	31

GROUP H. "HOPE" INSTRUCTIONS, "PUBLIC" EXPRESSION, "HIGH" DIFFICULTY CODE CHARACTERS

Trainee	Trial #1	Trial #2	Trial #3		Trial #4		Trial #5		Trial #6		Trial #7		Trial #8	
1	3	2	5	4	6	3	5	10	15	8	15	13	17	5
2	0	1	5	5	10	7	10	7	10	6	10	7	8	5
3	1	2	4	4	6	1	6	4	6	12	9	10	10	7
4	4	7	7	7	8	10	10	7	10	9	10	9	10	11
5	3	7	5	10	10	10	12	10	12	14	13	12	13	10
6	9	8	7	9	9	8	9	9	9	10	10	14	11	13
7	5	2	6	5	7	3	7	7	8	9	12	12	15	11
8	2	5	10	7	6	6	6	10	8	10	10	12	11	11
9	5	7	8	8	9	10	11	13	13	13	14	13	15	9
10	8	6	7	8	8	8	9	10	13	8	10	11	12	10

Trainee	Trial #9		Trial #10		Trail #11		Trial #12		Trial #13		Trial #14		Trial #15		Test Score
1	15	13	17	9	13	8	15	12	15	11	15	11	15	14	13
2	8	6	8	6	7	4	7	10	10	6	10	9	10	9	14
3	10	10	12	9	10	8	10	15	11	12	11	16	13	14	30
4	12	13	14	9	14	5	14	13	14	10	14	13	15	13	14
5	13	11	13	8	13	9	10	7	8	7	7	10	11	17	37
6	12	12	12	11	11	13	12	10	12	10	12	14	13	11	21
7	15	8	15	10	15	14	15	11	15	12	15	13	15	10	19
8	11	11	12	13	13	13	13	13	13	13	13	11	13	8	24
9	15	12	15	10	13	11	13	10	13	12	13	14	15	13	21
10	12	8	12	6	12	12	13	10	13	11	13	10	12	10	14

GROUP I. KNOWLEDGE OF RESULTS ALONE, "LOW" DIFFICULTY
CODE CHARACTERS

Trainee	Trial #1	Trial #2	Trial #3	Trial #4	Trial #5	Trial #6	Trial #7	Trial #8
1	11	13	19	15	15	15	16	13
2	19	16	19	19	17	20	20	17
3	11	11	12	13	19	16	17	18
4	11	14	15	14	11	13	12	19
5	8	14	15	13	13	15	13	16
6	15	11	9	17	20	20	19	20
7	7	9	6	11	10	13	11	11
8	8	12	9	9	8	16	13	11
9	9	8	6	12	13	13	11	10
10	4	9	5	9	7	9	4	11

Trainee	Trial #9	Trial #10	Trial #11	Trial #12	Trial #13	Trial #14	Trial #15	Test Score
1	16	15	17	17	20	19	18	27
2	20	21	21	22	22	21	20	41
3	23	21	23	24	18	24	23	42
4	15	21	19	18	20	15	16	39
5	17	16	14	18	14	17	16	31
6	18	20	19	16	22	23	21	43
7	7	8	11	8	9	15	16	27
8	15	14	14	10	15	17	14	25
9	15	14	11	16	11	14	14	29
10	5	6	5	3	3	7	5	9

Trainee	Trial #1	Trial #2	Trial #3	Trial #4	Trial #5	Trial #6	Trial #7	Trial #8
1	8	3	4	5	3	3	1	8
2	5	4	1	3	8	6	6	3
3	4	3	2	6	8	7	7	7
4	3	5	1	5	7	6	7	5
5	7	4	7	8	9	7	8	10
6	4	7	6	5	7	7	8	9
7	7	5	5	6	3	4	5	6
8	9	11	7	10	12	11	15	13
9	7	9	2	6	6	8	9	6
10	4	6	3	4	2	8	6	5

Trainee	Trial #9	Trial #10	Trial #11	Trial #12	Trial #13	Trial #14	Trial #15	Test Score
1	10	6	3	5	5	4	5	13
2	8	10	7	5	5	6	9	12
3	6	4	7	11	10	14	9	16
4	1	6	6	7	8	4	4	10
5	8	12	9	7	9	12	11	16
6	9	9	11	10	9	10	11	14
7	6	5	10	5	6	5	7	6
8	15	17	22	21	18	23	21	45
9	8	6	9	7	9	4	6	12
10	8	7	6	4	9	6	10	10

Bartlett's Test for Homogeneity of Variance of Performance Scores for the Five Criteria

Criterion	df	Chi-square value	χ^2
Block 1			
(sum trials 4 → 7)	7	11.249	14.067
Block 2			
(sum trials 8 → 11)	7	9.564	14.067
Block 3			
(sum trials 12 → 15)	7	11.824	14.067
Block 4			
(sum trials 6 → 15)	7	11.422	14.067
Test score	7	7.141	14.067

Analysis of Unadjusted Y (Performance Scores) for the Five Criteria Heading Each Table

Source	SS	df	MS	F	$F_{0.001}$
Block 1 Criterion					
Between groups	19,394.00	7	2,770.57	15.066	4.370
Within groups	13,239.80	72	183.89	—	—
Total	32,633.80	79			
Block 2 Criterion					
Between groups	20,938.55	7	2,991.22	13.579	4.370
Within groups	15,861.00	72	220.29	—	—
Total	36,799.55	79			
Block 3 Criterion					
Between groups	20,043.99	7	2,863.43	14.064	4.370
Within groups	14,658.90	72	203.60	—	—
Total	34,702.89	79			
Block 4 Criterion					
Between groups	123,510.89	7	17,644.41	14.812	4.370
Within groups	85,770.50	72	1,191.26	—	—
Total	209,281.39	79			
Test Score Criterion					
Between groups	4,717.49	7	673.93	11.103	4.370
Within groups	4,370.50	72	60.70	—	—
Total	9,087.99	79			

Analysis of the Significance of Regression of the Performance Scores of the First Two Training Trials on the Five Criteria Heading Each Table

Source	SS	df	MS	F	$F_{0.001}$
Block 1 Criterion					
Reduction due to regression	8,288.87	1	8,288.87	118.87	11.97
Residuals	4,950.93	71	69.73	—	—
Total (within groups)	13,239.80	72			
Block 2 Criterion					
Reduction due to regression	5,279.91	1	5,279.91	35.43	11.97
Residuals	10,581.09	71	149.03	—	—
Total (within groups)	15,861.00	72			
Block 3 Criterion					
Reduction due to regression	3,535.79	1	3,535.79	22.57	11.97
Residuals	11,123.11	71	156.66	—	—
Total (within groups)	14,658.90	72			
Block 4 Criterion					
Reduction due to regression	31,051.24	1	31,051.24	40.29	11.97
Residuals	54,719.26	71	770.69	—	—
Total (within groups)	85,770.50	72			
Test Score Criterion					
Reduction due to regression	785.93	1	785.93	15.57	11.97
Residuals	3,584.57	71	50.49	—	—
Total (within groups)	4,370.50	72			

Analysis of Homogeneity of Regression of the Performance Scores of the First Two Training Trials on the Five Criteria Heading Each Table

Source	SS	df	MS	F	$F_{0.05}$
Block 1 Criterion					
Deviations from individual group regressions	4,724.17	64	73.394	—	—
Differences among group regressions	226.76	7	32.394	0.439	2.25
Total deviations from average regression within group	4,950.93	71			
Block 2 Criterion					
Deviations from individual group regressions	10,231.77	64	159.871	—	—
Differences among group regressions	349.32	7	49.903	0.312	2.25
Total deviations from average regression within group	10,581.09	71			
Block 3 Criterion					
Deviations from individual group regressions	10,450.61	64	163.291	—	—
Differences among group regressions	672.50	7	96.071	0.588	2.25
Total deviations from average regression within group	11,123.11	71			

Block 4 Criterion
    Deviations from individ-

ual group regressions	52,478.81	64	819.981	—	—
Differences among group					
regressions	2,240.45	7	320.064	0.390	2.25
Total deviations from average regression within group	54,719.26	71			

Test Score Criterion
    Deviations from individ-

ual group regressions	3,426.21	64	53.535	—	—
Differences among group					
regressions	158.36	7	22.623	0.423	2.25
Total deviations from average regression within group	3,584.57	71			